A Familys Fairytale Turned Upside Down

Melissa Woitula-Alberts

A Family's Fairytale Turned Upside Down

Melissa Woitula-Alberts

Mockingbird Lane Press

A Family's Fairytale Turned Upside Down
Copyright © 2013 Melissa Woitula-Alberts

All rights reserved. No part of this book may be used or reproduced by any means, graphic, electronic, or mechanical, including photocopying, recording, taping or by any information storage retrieval system without the written permission of the publisher except in the case of brief quotations embodied in critical articles and reviews.

The publisher does not have any control over and does not assume any responsibility for author or third-party websites or their content.

Some names have been changed to protect the innocent.

Mockingbird Lane Press—Maynard, Arkansas
Library of Congress information in publishing data
ISBN: 978-0-9893105-0-5
0 9 8 7 6 5 4 3 2 1

Mockingbird Lane Press
www.mockinbirdlanepress.com
Cover Design by Jamie Johnson

This book is for all the teens that have voices to be heard. As their voices weaken to nonexistence, their innocence slowly becomes stripped and shredded while their lives become shattered and their journey is dark, as if living a nightmare that will not end.

Teenagers seem alive on the outside, but many are severely wounded and hurting on the inside for the truth to be heard. Their identity is tattered to shreds while anything that remains within feel like dirty rags that are useless and worthless. Countless numbers of our teens try anything to find out who they really are, where their identity lies within the family system and a place they call home.

There are many ways people lose identity—whether to mishaps in their childhood that leaves unbearable scars and an empty soul in need of healing.

Teens that have been battered and scarred will choose to carry the burden of every hurt, not knowing what true love is. It's unfortunate that the ones that said they cared and the authorities may have known what really happened, but are content to cover their eyes and ears to the truth while drowning out the crying voices. The rebellious behavior I experienced was my way of crying into the dark, desperate for someone to hear me.

This book is my way of telling all those who are hurting, desperate and in need of someone's attention that they are not alone.

Acknowledgements

To George Alberts, my best helpmate, friend, and husband of thirty years. I thank you for the emotional support you have given me to write and release my pain. You gave me encouragement that has lifted me up, keeping me on track.

To Sarah Alberts my daughter, whom at an early age had taught me to press on no matter what. Above all, Sarah's honesty to herself taught me to reach within the depths of my heart to search for my identity.

To Kathleen Woitula, my sister who is always learning and exploring the world around her. Without words, she could carefully direct me. She has taught me that hardships come only in our mind because the past is over.

To David (Woitula) Boltz, my younger brother. I praise the Lord for the time I have with you.

And to Anita Foster and lil' family.

I would also like to acknowledge others who have helped me along the way: Anita Foster, Yolanda Martin, Mary Platten, Bob and Anita Olsen, Lois Lemke, Todd Perrault, Jeri Raab, Dr. Leuthner, Gene Griffin, Dottie Cook, Dr. Gregory and wife Betty Gregory, Keith and Eva Carlisle and to my former co-workers at Harbour Suites and all the members of Great Harvest Church in Pocahontas, Arkansas.

Where does life begin and when does life end?
No one really knows.
How much does a mother and father love their daughter?
Only they will know.
How much does a daughter miss her mother and father?
Only she will know.

Chapter 1
Fairytales do not always have a happy ending, or do they?

~ What can I say; the devil stole my childhood so I would not fulfill God purpose for my life.~

~God made a promise to me and my Lord lives." ~

Once upon a time, a happy family lived in a wonderful neighborhood of DePere, Wisconsin. Summertime had officially arrived on that June 9, 1974. I was eagerly awaiting my fourteenth birthday with a special party Mom had arranged. It started as a typical summer with no warning of what was to come.

On that particular Sunday afternoon, my dad surprised us by suggesting a family outing—dinner at Eddie Whipp's Supper Club in Eaton, a few miles east of DePere.

Dad's excitement was contagious as he was eager to drive our new car. The white with gold pin stripes Chevy Chevelle was so different from the baby blue station wagon. A classy car. It was to be our first ride as a family and Mom, Dad, Kim, Russell, Monica, baby David and me, Missy, climbed into the car in anticipation, savoring the new car smell.

Eddie Whipp's Supper Club was a long, low building that used to be white, but now had a distinct grayish tinge to it. Inside the double doors, tables were scattered throughout the main area, a bar along the back wall and pinball machines in a far corner.

We sat at a long table, reminding me of our traditional Thanksgiving dinner. Once grace was said, we wasted no time filling our plates. We shared our thoughts, school events, admired how David was growing so big and Russell's summer job. Laughter hung over the table like a happy bubble, enfolding us in its safe cocoon. Mom and Dad, as usual, had a drink or two and my siblings and I sugared up on kiddie cocktails and were bouncing off the walls.

Dinner finished, Dad allowed us to play the pinball machine while he paid for the meal. While waiting my turn, I glanced toward the bar where Mom and Dad, drinks in hand, were talking to friends.

The perfect June day turned gray and dismal as we enjoyed our meal. Dark clouds hung in the sky and soft rain patterned the pavement. Standing in the rain in momentary confusion, Dad roared with laughter as he realized he still looked for our blue wagon.

Shuffling and pushing, Monica, Russell and I argued over the window seats in the back. As the oldest, Russell and I won, Monica drawing the hated middle.

Mom and Dad, of course, were in the front seat, Kim between them and David sitting on Mom's lap. (In 1974 seatbelts were not required and seldom used). In spite of the rain, we were full, contented and happy. Looking back in time, I would trade anything for that one moment. Just that one solitary moment when I could tell each of them how much I loved them.

Dad's new car slid gracefully onto the Highway 29 West. I could hear Dad humming with the repetition of the windshield wipers.

A Family's Fairytale Turned Upside Down

Monica turned to me to ask a question concerning cheerleading outing coming up. I'm sure I answered her, but seeing her face, half-shadowed, reminded me of a question I had asked her a few nights before my eighth grade graduation.

"Monica," I had said, while lying in bed, staring at a dark ceiling. "What would you do if I died?"

In the thick, eerie silence, I heard her small voice say, "I would be sad for a long time and I would miss you very much."

I remember turning over and crying myself to sleep. I shook off the dregs of that awful question as I smiled at her. Today was not the day to dwell on death. It was a day to enjoy being with my family and admiring our new car.

Tires whooshed along the wet pavement as Kim told Mom about her job as Nanny to a family in Green Bay. It was especially nice to be with Kim as she would be leaving as soon as we got home. The only thing that would have made this day even more perfect would have been if Kathy, our oldest sister, was here.

At the intersection of Highway 29 and Lily Lake Road, Mom suddenly screamed, "Joe!"

Before I could turn my head, something slammed into the side of our brand new car. Tortured metal shrieked as glass exploded, raining over us in crystal shards, drowning out the human screams. When the car came to a halt, I wavered in and out of consciousness, wondering what happened. The sound of raindrops on the roof was all I understood.

Dark. Inside and out. I couldn't see. Couldn't move. Blinking, my vision came into focus a little better, but the carnage in front of me was as though on a movie screen and I was a disinterested bystander. A strangled moan from the other side of the car echoed through the crushed metal.

"Russell? Russell? What happened?"

His hand found mine in the darkness. "Missy," he said, "just close your eyes."

I complied, but asked if David was okay.

A heavy moan answered me, then only silence except for the tick, tick of a cooling engine. I felt as if I should do something, but I had no idea what that might be.

"He's there," Russell finally said. "Right in front of you."

I located the baby, his whimpering pitiful and scary. If I could only reach him, I could hug the terror away. But I couldn't move. Just a foot away, I watched him crawl across Kim's back.

"Kim," I said. "Take David. Please make him stop crying."

"She can't," Russell whispered.

My eyes sought my sister hunched over in the seat. She didn't move as David pushed and pulled his way across her. Her head dangled, curly blond hair saturated with a thick, black substance I couldn't identify.

David's striped shirt and navy blue corduroy overalls had been painted from head to foot in the same thing that covered Kim. The smell of copper filled my nostrils; a metallic taste coated my tongue. Dizziness washed over me.

I managed to reach out to Russell, shaking his arm anxiously. "What is that stuff on David?"

In a strangled voice, he said, "It's blood, Missy. It's all over."

My eyes landed on Monica sitting beside me. Her head had fallen forward, and blood dripped from her nose and from her eyes, staining her cheeks in black tears. Blood? My God, so much of it.

In my mind, I screamed for Daddy, but no words came. I wanted him to enfold me in his strong arms and assure me it was just a nightmare. Everything would be okay. But Daddy wasn't going to hold me or reassure me about anything. His head, covered in blood was smashed against the windshield, staining the glass in a dark rose tint.

Somehow, deep inside, I knew they were all dead, but I simply couldn't comprehend this horror. I do remember looking at Monica again and thinking, I'm going to be sad for a very long time and I will miss you very much.

The scene around me unfolded like a "B" horror movie. Camera lens quick images captured horrific, unforgiving images that would haunt me for the rest of my life. I wanted to check on my mother, but I couldn't bring myself to do so. The world as I knew it had exploded in a black bloody haze.

Blinding lights from other vehicles on the highway, along with flashing lights, lit the inside of the car with a macabre dance of light and shadow. As they screeched to a halt, people poured out of their cars and wandered around us, looking in, while trying to console. I wondered why they weren't helping—weren't making this awful thing go away.

Meaningless words drifted through splintered glass. "Everything will be okay. Hang in there. An ambulance is coming."

They lied. Nothing would ever be all right again.

Police cars filled my line of vision while the talk amongst them and the bystanders became louder—nothing but jumbled words that made no sense to me.

As the EMT's approached the car and pried open the passenger side door, I saw my mother slump toward them. I knew at that moment something other than a car accident was happening to me, but I couldn't explain it then and I can't explain it today. Someone or something took over my mind and body, leaving me trapped forever in a brand new, but battered Chevy Chevelle.

Maslow's Hierarchy of needs

```
              /\
             /SELF-\
            /ACTUALIZATION\
           /Pursue Inner Talent\
          /Creativity Fulfillment\
         /------------------------\
        /      SELF-ESTEEM         \
       /   Achievement Mastery      \
      /    Recognition Respect       \
     /--------------------------------\
    /       BELONGING - LOVE           \
   /     Friends Family Spouse Lover    \
  /--------------------------------------\
 /              SAFETY                    \
/   Security Stability Freedom from Fear   \
/--------------------------------------------\
/              PHYSIOLOGICAL                  \
/        Food Water Shelter Warmth             \
------------------------------------------------
```

Prior to the accident, my life strongly displayed the Maslow's Hierarchy of needs, all five were evident, and the triangle was complete. First, my Physiological needs were met; I never went without food, water, shelter, and warmth. Second, I always felt safe; I had no fear of the world around me, the feeling of security and protection of my home and family remained strong and stable. Third, I always felt as I belonged in my family unit with love. I carried a strong sense of belonging within my network of friends. Fourth, my self-esteem was high, due to the acceptance of my friends, neighborhood, school and family. Fifth, self-actualization, I played the piano and flute, sang in the school choir, always exploring various activities in and out of school. It was evident that I was open-minded to my surroundings.

Middle and late childhood (7-12 years)

- **Hopes: Trust vs. Mistrust** (Oral-sensory, Birth-2 years)

- **Existential Question: Can I Trust the World?**

The first stage of Erik Erikson's theory centers around the infant's basic needs being met by the parents. If the parents surround the child to warmth, regularity, and dependable affection, the infant's view of the world will be one of trust. Should the parents fail to provide a secure environment and to meet the child's basic needs a sense of mistrust will result. Development of mistrust can lead to feelings of frustration, suspicion, withdrawal, and a lack of confidence.

Chapter 2
Innocence of a Little Girl

~What is good; is having a childhood that brings many good memories. The kind that allow time to fall back, where it can be seen, heard, felt, heard, smelled and tasted as if it were yesterday~

Like arrows piercing my face, raindrops fell from an unforgiving sky. Once they'd lifted my mother from the car, the EMT's turned to me. I crawled out of the car on my own, pushing helpful hands away as I walked to the ambulance, shoulders straight, head high. It was in my mind that nothing could hurt me from that moment on—I could handle anything that came my way. How little I knew. But shock, total and debilitating, threw up an impenetrable wall around me and I felt nothing.

Bits and pieces of the accident flashed through my mind so fast I couldn't hold on to any particular image. Not that I wanted to. I wanted the last few hours to go away—I *wanted* to be home with my family. The ride to the hospital was equally blank. I vaguely recall the sound of sirens and flashing lights, but I don't remember anything else until I woke up hours later.

When I tried to focus my attention on what was happening around me, all I saw was a scarlet colored mist clouding my vision and in my nostrils, the coppery smell of death.

Sometime during the night, other smells finally penetrated. The odor of disinfectant, vomit, medicine and an underlying aroma of urine overwhelmed me. I knew from that, I was in a hospital, but I had no idea where or why.

Doctors and nurses scurried to fulfill mysterious missions. I got out of bed and stood next to a large white graph board that looked as cold and alone as I felt. At one point, I managed to waylay a nurse long enough to ask why I was there and where they'd put my clothes.

She paused to say, "You're in St. Vincent's Hospital in Green Bay. You were in a car accident." She gave me a tentative smile.

"Where's my family?"

The smile dropped from her face as she gently patted my arm, "Don't worry, I'll take good care of you," she said, hurrying away.

My mind whirled with questions. I wanted to know where my family was, what had happened and why Mom and Dad weren't here with me. I went back to the ER cubicle and crawled into bed.

While I lay there, scared, alone and confused, Dad's brother, who'd shared so many fun weekends and memories, walked in. For a second, relief flooded my body. He would give me the answers I so desperately needed.

That feeling didn't last long. "Where's Mom and Dad?" I asked, my hands clutching the bed railings so tight my knuckles turned white.

He burst into tears, unable to meet my eyes. "They're gone," he said.

"Gone where?"

A Family's Fairytale Turned Upside Down

Without answering, he walked away, leaving a terrified and heartbroken little girl to fend for herself with no one to comfort her.

Not long after my uncle's visit, they moved me upstairs. Lying in that stark white room, I tried not to think about what was happening to me. The sounds came back first—screaming, shattering glass. Car accident. Had any of my family survived? My tears soaked the rough white pillowcase.

My heart leapt as my fifteen-year-old brother, Russell was wheeled into the room. Whether glad to see him or out of fear, I'm not sure. He lay in a bed, wires, pulleys and metal bars protruding everywhere. This wasn't my brother; this was a monster straight out of my nightmares. Plaster casts covered his legs from crotch to toes and wires held them immobile as they positioned his bed next to mine. I had barely gotten over the shock when they rolled David into the room in a baby bed. He laid so still, bandages around his abdomen and head. Tears trickled down my cheeks as I watched them both.

When Russell awoke a few hours later, we talked, but neither of us had any answers. Russell tried to prepare me for the reality that the other members of our family in that car had died, but I didn't want to hear it. Exhausted, I fell into a fitful sleep.

I awoke sometime later to a roomful of aunts and uncles. In my mind, I played out the hopeful fantasies that Mom and Dad were hurt, but would be okay and my sisters as well. My heart couldn't bear any other answers. Russell's eyes met mine and I knew he had the same soul-destroying thoughts that I did.

Then the bombed dropped. My parents, Joe and Peggy, my sisters Kim and Monica were gone—just like that. God snapped his fingers and took them from me and this world in a split second.

Not only would my life never be the same, *I* would never be the same. Something inside me died that day along with my parents and sisters. How is it possible to prepare a person, especially a child for the devastating news that half the family had been wiped out in an instant? That they had died when *I* had walked away.

Why the three of us survived is not a question with a ready-made answer. Over the years, I've heard, "It was God's will." Of course it was God's will, but how do you explain that to a child?

I thought families stayed together, growing old, living and loving, sharing our lives with each other, our children and grandchildren. Where was the justice in leaving children behind with no one to comfort them? Not one of the aunts or uncles bothered with hugs or assurances everything would be okay. They chatted amongst themselves as though the three refugees weren't in the room. Because that's what we were—surviving refugees that no one wanted.

Nor did they stay long, leaving my brother and me to deal as best we could. So many tears were shed once the three of us were alone. David, too little to understand what was happening, cried because Russell and I were. I shriveled inside like a fish lying on the desert floor.

My older sister, Kathy, had left home—let's be honest—she ran away from home so many times, she was finally placed with a foster family and as I lay in bed, I wondered where she was and why she wasn't there to make things better. At twenty-one she was at least more of an adult than Russell and I. Maybe she could help us sort this all out. But she didn't come and I was left feeling abandoned once again.

When I had asked my aunts and uncles where she was, they informed me rather quickly that she was a bad influence and I would do well to stay away from her. It didn't matter to me that Kathy was more or less a hippie, that she ran away to live her own life, I knew that she loved us and would be there if she could.

My injuries, a doctor informed me, were minor. Russell's legs were broken in several places, which would keep him in the hospital for many months. Little David suffered head, abdominal and chest injuries, but nothing life threatening.

Why was I spared? I couldn't understand why God didn't take me as well. Even though I didn't want to die, I couldn't help thinking it would be better than this pain—this loneliness—this emptiness.

Exhaustion, shock or both allowed me to sleep. As I drifted off, I imagined God had sent four angels—the biggest and brightest of them all to wrap their wings around us in love and comfort.

The following morning, when I refused help from the nurses to go to the bathroom, I didn't know it was a form of controlling what happened around me. Nor did I realize I was plagued with survivor's guilt that would haunt me for years to come.

On Wednesday, three days after the accident, we were told about the funeral. My doctor said I was well enough to attend, but to return immediately. I couldn't do it. I didn't want the memory of those four caskets in my head. I didn't want the sad funeral music, or the smell of decaying flowers—of death lingering in my mind. I had had enough death to last me a lifetime.

My mother's smile became a cherished memory I clung to. I wanted to keep the feel of Dad's strong arms around me and the feel of my sister's hands in mine. Not the sight of them lying there cold and "gone."

To this day, I know I made the right choice. I refused to do what others told me was right and acceptable and made my own decision, the only way I knew how.

As I lay in the hospital bed, to keep my mind off my family being lowered into the dark, cold ground, I thought instead of my birthday. Like all special occasions, birthdays for a child, holds magic and wonder. Mom made us feel that our day was the best day of all. When we would awaken, there would always be a wrapped gift or two at the foot of our bed. What a way to start a special day. Mom told us that on our birthday, we were King or Queen for the day; a special day for the birthday boy or girl.

The homemade cake Mom made was usually lopsided and the frosting dripped down the sides, but to me, it was the most beautiful cake in the world. Since my birthday was on the 14th, it was also Flag Day. Flags in our neighborhood began to sprout from lawns and porches in preparation for the patriotic day. I thought they were for my birthday.

A Family's Fairytale Turned Upside Down

Mom agreed. "Missy," she said, "all of America loves you and are joining in to celebrate your special day." Kim, the know-it-all, was quick to set me straight, but Mom's words comforted me now. It would be nice to think that all of America loved me so much they would put flags out.

On my last birthday, Mom, her sweet smile directed at me said, "What would you like most out of life?"

"To be a mother just like you and have a family. I want to be just like you."

I remember the warmth, the comfort and most of all, the love she imparted as she gathered me in her arms, eyes tearing up as she hugged me.

Fairytale? Yes, to me, it certainly was. No family is without arguments, disagreements or anger, but in spite of the occasional bad times, we all knew we were loved.

After the funeral, reporters descended on us like locusts in a corn field. I was so embarrassed and ashamed as they scrutinized me in that horrible gown with the slit down the back.

They asked impossible questions, such as, "How do you feel?"

"What do you remember of the accident?"

"Was your dad drunk?"

"What will you do now that your parents are gone?"

Reeling with shock and the knowledge we would never see part of our family again, ones we'd not gotten to say goodbye to or I love you, kept us quiet as the questions bombarded us like cannons on a battlefield.

Why these people were allowed in I'll never know. To this day, I still ask why someone didn't prevent them from coming, or stop them in the process. Didn't they know neither Russell nor I was equipped to handle such questions and accusations?

In the meantime, it was decided the three of us would live with an aunt and uncle. As our uncle said, "Where else are they to go?"

Once upon a time, a happy family lived in a wonderful neighborhood of De Pere Wisconsin…but then, the wicked witch of fate turned it into a nightmare.

Will: Autonomy vs. Shame & Doubt (Muscular-Anal, 2-4 years)
- **Existential Question: Is It OK to Be Me?**

As the child gains control over eliminative functions and motor abilities, they begin to explore their surroundings. The parents still provide a strong base of security from which the child can venture out to assert their will. The parents' patience and encouragement helps foster autonomy in the child. At this age children develop their first interests. For example, a child who enjoys music may like to play with the radio. Highly restrictive parents, however, are more likely to instill in the child a sense of doubt, and reluctance to attempt new challenges.

If caregivers encourage self-sufficient behavior, toddlers develop a sense of autonomy—a sense of being able to handle many problems on their own. But if caregivers demand too much too soon, refuse to let children perform tasks of which they are capable, or ridicule early attempts at self-sufficiency, children may instead develop shame and doubt about their ability to handle problems.

Chapter 3
Take it all 'til there is nothing left

~We had joy, we had fun, we had seasons in the sun but the wine and the song like the seasons have all gone...~

I was released from the hospital the day I turned fourteen. Instead of Queen for the day, I was just one more lost young girl trying to understand, to find my way in a world I wasn't sure I belonged in.

I thought about the decorations Mom had already bought; stacked on the kitchen counter, ready to transform an everyday house into a magical castle just for me. A few of my friends tried to make it a good day, stopping by the hospital with a cake to celebrate the best way they knew how. I appreciated their efforts, but it only reminded me of what should have been—not this nightmarish reality.

When I was told I could go home, I asked the nurse why I had to leave. I wanted to stay with Russell and David and here, I had no decisions to make, no place to be.

"Because you're well enough to go home. You don't need to be here,"

To leave my brothers filled me with such loneliness I couldn't breathe. It was as though they were being taken from me as well. Anger toward God and the drunk driver who had hit us, guilt for having survived fought for dominance in my mind. I didn't know what to feel or how to handle it. As I clung to Russell, I knew I was also abandoning them both, just as my parents and sisters had abandoned us all.

Watching Russell, held captive by the monster chaining him to the bed, I wanted to take away his pain—his and David's. I wanted to turn back time when the fairytale was alive and well.

Instead, I did as Russell and I had agreed. To do as we were told, make no waves, to do the best we could. I raged at God. Why? How could you let this happen? What had we done to deserve this? Why was I spared? Why was Russell given so much physical pain while I endured an emotional breakdown? At the time, I didn't know Russell was doing his own raging.

We hugged, cried and reassured each other it would be all right. Letting them go took every ounce of strength I had, both physically and emotionally. My first step to the door was mind-numbing. I looked back. The image of that pitiful, lonely and damaged young man lying in that big white bed would prey on my mind for years.

Walking down the corridor, no one said a word. The distraught look on the nurse's faces was evident this was not going to turn out well. Many glanced up from their clipboards and desks and some even managed a smile. One offered good wishes. But my luck had died on Highway 29 and there was no getting it back.

As I approached the exit doors, I had full knowledge I was stepping into a world where evil lived and drunks crawled into cars that maimed and killed.

As the doors whooshed open, a dark-haired lady came toward me. For a split second, she reminded me of my mother and I smiled. Instantly, I realized it wasn't, couldn't be her, could never be her.

At that moment, I retreated to a hollow place, empty and devoid of emotion. Guilt and shame filled my heart and there was no room for anything else.

A few days ago, I was a member of a happy family. Today I was an orphaned child with no one to turn to. My life had crashed as sure as those two cars connected and I was left with only memories.

Survivor's Guilt: The emotion of guilt is associated with the realization or perception of wrongdoing (of having violated an important social, moral, or ethical rule; Chaplin, 1975). A person may feel guilty without being consciously aware of it. Conscious and unconscious guilt may act as an underlying factor in behavior, emotions and relationships. Although conscious guilt is experiences as very real, a distinction has been made between "real" (or active) guilt and "imagined" (or passive) guilt (Danieli, 1984; Lifton, 1993). Following traumatic events, an individual may experience "real" guilt for acts of commission or omission that resulted in the physical or emotional endangerment or harm of others. "Imagined" guilt (e.g. survivor guilt, guilt with an element of wishful thinking about one's ability to act) includes the type of guilt that occur in the absence of having acted harmfully. Both types of guilt include condemnation, and either can result in harm to self or others (e.g, punishing acts to self or others; the action or elicitation of rejection, disdain and/or punishment).

Chapter 4
Lost Identity

~An identity lies deep within me; I do not know which one I am today. I will wait to discover what role I should play depending on my surroundings. It has become easy to camouflage the truth: I don't know what truth is.~

The relatives who felt obligated to take the poor little orphan girl, walked with me to the car. Once settled in the back seat, my hands shook and a cold sweat beaded my forehead as it dawned on me I sat in the same spot the night my world crashed around me in screeching metal and shattering glass. I steeled myself, not wanting my aunt and uncle to know how badly it affected me. I tuned everything out and simply endured the interminable ride.

In spite of my determination, thoughts of my birthday crept in. Today should have been a flurry of activity as we prepared for the party. Mom and I talked, argued, laughed and bubbled with excitement. The only thing she refused to discuss was my cake. As the tires hummed over the pavement, I wondered what kind of cake she'd ordered. Now I would never know and I felt another piece of my heart break away.

On my way to a familiar, yet unknown destination with no clear vision of what my future held, I couldn't help but once again ask why? Why had my family been taken from me? So many questions, so few answers. My safe haven gone, I was now dependant on family members that I knew didn't want me.

A Family's Fairytale Turned Upside Down

I swallowed back the tears. I didn't want to think anymore, didn't want my mother's excited giggle in my head. My new home was exactly how I imaged it to be. Lonely.

A few days later, they took me back to my house to retrieve some of my belongings. As we drove, I overheard them talking about getting the house emptied as soon as possible so they could sell it. My heart shattered in my chest. My family was gone, my home soon to follow. What would I have left? Nothing but memories, shame, guilt and fear.

My first inclination was to scream at them; to tell them it wasn't their house to sell. They had no right to sell my mother's beautiful red refrigerator she'd been so proud of. But I also knew it wouldn't do any good. If I'd heard it once, I'd heard it a thousand times in the past few days—"It's for your own good."

The drive to the house was torment. I couldn't imagine walking through the door and my mother not being there to welcome me home with a smile and hug. Not to see my dad sitting in his recliner, catching a baseball game, yelling as his team scored. Or Monica's bubbly voice wafting down the staircase as she played a rowdy game with her Barbie dolls. I couldn't do it. I couldn't face the silent emptiness.

As we pulled into the driveway, I didn't throw up or run away screaming. Like everything else since the accident, it was something that had to be endured, so I steeled myself and got out of the car.

I wondered what happened to Rufus, the little dog we'd gotten only a few weeks before. When I asked, my aunt said they'd had it put down because he was a biter. Rufus was a good dog and I knew unless someone treated him badly, he wouldn't have bit anyone. One more loss I wasn't equipped to handle.

Inside, I walked past treasured possessions, aching to touch everything in my path. Fear stilled my hands. Deep down, I was afraid if I touched them, they too, would disappear.

Each item had a memory attached to it and I fought hard to keep them at bay. The memories were mine alone to grab hold of while carefully storing them in my heart to tend when I needed to.

In the living room was the shelf where we had placed baby Jesus in special tissue paper to be placed in the manger on Christmas morning. It seemed as if I could hear the strains of Dad's records as he listened to Burl Ives, Sing Along With Mitch and Pat Boone. In the corner would be the Christmas tree, piled high with presents, excitement rampant as we impatiently waited for that wonderful day, trying to guess what Mom and Dad had gotten us.

In the room my dad used when he came home late from work, I gathered his pillow in my arms, inhaling his scent one last time. Memories of his laughter, the fun we'd had all came rushing back and my tears mingled with the scent on the pillow.

In my parent's bedroom, Mom's perfume, jewelry and trinkets sat on the dresser as though she would walk through the door any second to put them to use. Staring at her clothes in the closet, it really hit me. I'd never hear her voice, see her smile or feel her arms around me again. I gathered her dresses to me and let the tears come yet again. I could still see her sitting in the comfortable chair in the living room, a book by her favorite author, Alfred Hitchcock in her hands as she concentrated on the words. As I stood there, I could almost hear her singing *Puff the Magic Dragon*, our favorite song. I wasn't sure I would be able to walk out of this house on my own steam.

In mine and Monica's room, the pain of loss hit me again. Her school books lay on the desk where she'd left them. Her toys and Barbie dolls lined a shelf by her bed. The book she was reading lay opened on the bed, a book she'd never get to finish. Memories of us outside on a summer night came rushing back. We'd play One o'lock, Two o'clock, Three o'clock Midnight, Swing the Statue, Simon Says and Kick the Can. Sometimes we'd play Double Dutch if we didn't have two people to turn the rope, we'd use a chair to hold one end.

Monica and I were only eleven months apart and we were as close as twins. We called her Bird because she was so little and delicate.

I turned my back to her things and went to my closet. While digging through it to see what I wanted to keep, I came across my trinket box and opened it. The faint smell of rotten egg wafted out. Every Easter, Mom bought eggs to color and I loved the ones that cracked while boiling. When we dyed them, color seeped onto the smooth egg white, a psychedelic swirl of bright colors. One year a particularly colorful egg caught my attention; it was so beautiful. I took it upstairs, holding it carefully lest I drop it. I placed the egg into the trinket box, gently closing the lid. A couple months later, rotten egg aroma permeated the room. I'd had to throw the once beautiful egg away, but even through a long airing period, the odor remained.

While I hadn't thrown my family away, it was as though, they too, had rotted away, leaving a stench in my nostrils I could never erase.

My sense of belonging evaporated with my tears. I was a stranger in my own home, about to embark on an adventure that had been forced upon me and one I didn't want.

I can't say exactly how I left the house where we'd been so happy. I became an automaton, simply placing one foot in front of the other, doing what I was told. The following days melded together and I waded through the best I could.

Relatives said later that they were trying to protect me. But when you're told to "get over it" they are telling you to bury the pain. Buried pain manifests itself in other ways, and most are not good. Just because you can bury it doesn't mean it doesn't still hurt or it's out of sight. It just festers and becomes a sore that won't heal. But I buried it like they suggested and I rebelled however I could.

I found myself obsessing over that fateful day. Could I have done something differently that afternoon to change the course of events? If I'd lingered just five minutes longer at the pinball machine, maybe the drunk driver would have wrecked only his car. It became a game—what could I have done to change the devastating events—to imagine ways to delay our departure. Would it have made a difference? Possibly. But I've learned through the years, you can't change the past. You can only do the best you can to go forward, no matter how hard it may be.

During this time, I received a letter from Caroline, whom I'd never met, but her letter was so sweet. She'd heard about my family and tried to reach out, giving me someone to communicate with. I did write her back a few times, but I was at a loss as to what I should say and so distrustful of people by this time that the letters fell by the wayside.

Yes, I lost my family that day, but as the weeks passed, I began to lose my identity and my self-worth. I walked through the hours with little interest in everyday life and became a ghost floating through a space I no longer cared to occupy.

Fidelity: Identity vs. Role Confusion (Adolescence, 13-19 years)

- **Existential Question: Who Am I and What Can I Be?**

The adolescent is newly concerned with how they appear to others. In later stages of Adolescence, the child develops a sense of sexual identity. As they make the transition from childhood to adulthood, adolescents ponder the roles they will play in the adult world. Initially, they are apt to experience some role confusion—mixed ideas and feelings about the specific ways in which they will fit into society—and may experiment with a variety of behaviors and activities (e.g. tinkering with cars, baby-sitting for neighbors, affiliating with certain political or religious groups). Eventually, Erikson proposed, most adolescents achieve a sense of identity regarding who they are and where their lives are headed.

Erikson is credited with coining the term "Identity Crisis." Each stage that came before and that follows has its own 'crisis', but even more so now, for this marks the transition from childhood to adulthood. But the need for identity in youth is not met by these." This emerging sense of self will be established by 'forging' past experiences with anticipations of the future.

Chapter 5
I should have died with them

~When my physiological, safety, love and belonging, self-esteem and self-actualization dissolved, I had nothing to live for.~

Teenage years are the best years of your life. Whoever said that hadn't a clue. Maybe if my family hadn't died, those *would* have been the best years, but under the circumstances, I lived in a waking nightmare.

David, released from the hospital, came to live with us. It gave me some comfort to have one family member with me, even though it would be temporary, because I knew my aunt and uncle wouldn't keep him. I grew hard and unrelenting. Every now and then, I would intercept the glares from my aunt and uncle and I was discouraged from picking David up and holding him close. Each time I tried, my aunt would unceremoniously take him from me. Eventually, he learned to whisper his disappointments and hurt feelings to me so no one else would hear him.

My friends were gone as well. My girlfriends and I started a club called "The Bubblegum Club," and we'd met in my garage every week. Cindy, Lisa, Elizabeth and several others had been very good friends and done everything together, including sleepovers where we talked about sex. That's where I learned what little I knew. It sure wasn't talked about in our house and I knew almost nothing. But my girlfriends, whether right or wrong, provided me with an education about the birds and bees. The new school year, I would be attending a new school, starting all over again. I wanted the old me, but I stayed withdrawn and broken. I had lost too much and I refused to put my heart out there to be broken yet again.

Several times through the following weeks, I would take the bus to the hospital to see Russell, gathering my nerve to face the monster that held him captive. It was good to be with him knowing we shared the same pain and abandonment issues. Yet, there was a reserve between us now neither of us could bridge.

It was a bittersweet day when he joined David and me. Cousins teased him and called him names and I could see the same withdrawal in Russell's eyes that I saw every morning in the mirror.

Four cousins resented our intrusion. The small house grew smaller, fraught with tension and confusion. Words not said hurt the most and the conversations felt stilted and fake.

Even David turned against me with hateful words when I tried to hug him. Trying to maintain a relationship with Russell was tantamount to betraying the "other" family's feelings and we learned quickly to walk a quiet line. Little by little, I gave up.

I desired the pity I felt I deserved, but didn't get. I was fourteen, unable to put things in perspective and understand the emotions and thoughts of others. If I had died with my family, I'm not sure anyone would have cared. I was an unwelcome intruder.

Not long after the accident, I was sitting on the bed in the bedroom I shared with my cousin, near tears and lonely. Another aunt came in the room, glaring at me.

"It's been over three months now. It's time to stop sniveling. It's time to get over it."

After she left, I thought back through those long three months. When had anyone asked me how I was doing? Where were the hugs? Why didn't anyone wipe away my tears when I cried? No one bothered to ask if I wanted to talk about it. I felt smothered in everyone else's emotions and not allowed to express mine. How do you get over losing four family members at the same time? How was a fourteen-year-old, who had lived a sheltered life, expected to "get over" such a travesty.

I had no one to tell me about the changes my body was going through. My aunt barely spoke to me and when she did, it was short and snappy. I was upset because I had started my period and didn't know why, how it would affect me or what to expect.

I walked to the city park and was sitting on a bench when Bill, a park worker came up to me. I'd met him before and he was always nice to the kids. He sat down beside me and asked what was wrong. It all came rushing out. I'm not sure I could have stopped even if I wanted to. I was so lost and confused about everything.

Very gently, he explained what having a period meant, the changes my body would go through and what to expect. He told me about the facts of life that day, something no one else had bothered to do. Looking back, I realize how sad it was for a teenage girl to learn about her bodily functions from a city park worker. But I shall be forever grateful to him.

In the fall of 1974, I was required to go to court regarding my aunt and uncle's guardianship. Humiliation filled me as the authorities displayed me in front of the courtroom as a specimen of death. The stench of other's offenses became a stigma attached to me like a disease.

I saw no point in the procedure as I was allowed to say little. My uncle became our Guardian at litem (GAL) to represent our best interest. Our best interest would have been better served had they allowed Kathy to become our Guardian and taken us home where we could have at least felt we belonged. But no. Kathy was a non-person, someone they talked about in whispered conversations they didn't want us to hear.

She had been allowed to see me for a few minutes about seven or eight days after the funeral. I was told she was no good and I should avoid her. But I loved her and I knew that she had tried to take the three of us. To be a responsible adult and help us adjust to the unexpected turn in our lives. She wasn't fit, according to my aunt and uncle, to raise any child, much less three.

Russell and I had to appear before a lawyer who asked us questions like, "How much had your dad had to drink the day of the accident? Do you think he was drunk? Did he drink a lot at home? Question after question was fired at us as we sat, stunned and confused. Dad hadn't caused the accident, why were they asking about it? We didn't know why, but finally, I couldn't take it anymore and stormed from the room, Russell behind me. How dare they try to put this all on Dad. We were having a good time that day, and yes, he'd had a drink or two, but he wasn't drunk and this wasn't his fault. He would never have put us in that kind of danger. But doubts did creep into my mind in spite of my certainty Dad would never have gotten behind the wheel if he thought he would put his family in danger. One more thing to thank the authorities for.

The first Memorial Day came and the family bundled everyone up for a trip to the cemetery. For Russell and I, it was a trip straight to hell. I knew, God how I knew, my family was gone, but seeing those headstones lined up beside each other, names engraved so preciously—brought it home more than anything else could. It took everything I had not to lay down on Mom's grave and beg them to leave me there. To go on without them wasn't something I felt prepared to do. I didn't, of course, I held my head high, refusing to cry in front of my aunts and uncles, refusing to show any weakness, because I knew they would jump on it like a lion attacks a gazelle. And I wanted them having no more ammunition than possible where I was concerned. They already resented me; I didn't want to make it worse.

Nervous about entering 9th grade in a new school where I knew no one but the cousins who ignored me most of the time, I would walk down the snowy sidewalk, turn around and look at my footprints. If they looked straight and perfect, I would be satisfied; however, if crooked or out of line, I would chastise myself and try harder. I didn't realize it at the time, but it was a way to control and to be perfect—the child someone would want and love.

I didn't feel as smart as the other kids and that kept me from pushing myself forward to make friends. Plus I gained weight and the kids laughed at me. I withdrew from the social scene, staying by myself and getting through each day. If I didn't talk to anyone, then I wouldn't be hurt by their mean comments.

Russell didn't stay with us long. Conflict day after day with our relatives helped in the decision that it would be better for him in a foster home. Although Russell and I were no longer as close as we used to be, I couldn't help but remember the afternoon at my grandparent's house on the bay when Russell talked me into getting in a rowboat. I did and he pushed it away from shore. I didn't worry too much until I realized there were no paddles in the boat. Russell, thinking it was too funny, let me suffer for awhile before he brought the raft out to rescue me. Oh, how I wanted that Russell back. I felt I had lost yet another family member and was about to lose David as well. I knew we weren't wanted in this over-filled home and it was also time for me to leave—to start over once again.

Aware that I might never see my brothers again, I closed my heart even more. So much, so, that it made very little difference whether they stayed or not. I wanted us all to go home, to be as we once were, but that being impossible, I felt any place would be better than where I was.

I would be leaving in February 1976. Icy attitudes swept through the house; snarls and unspoken words pierced my heart, and my emotions were tangled into a black tumor of dread.

The night before I was to leave inched by; minutes feeling like hours. I couldn't sleep and memories overwhelmed me.

Every spring, we'd go to Kewaunee, a small town that lay along the bay. In the evening, Dad would get together with family and friends to go smelt fishing. Smelt were little fish

A Family's Fairytale Turned Upside Down

you caught in a huge net so big it took two men to pull it in. Dad's friend, Bucky, was the one to usually help. I remembered the sound of Dad's voice as he yelled, "The run is on!"

Dad, in his waders, cigarette dangling from his lips, would walk into the water, slowly pulling the net. Afterward, we'd have a huge fish fry with friends, neighbors and family.

Dad worked for Fore Way Express as a truck driver. When he'd leave for work and I was on my bicycle, I would pedal as fast as I could, yelling, "Wait Daddy! Wait! I need to give you a goodbye kiss."

He always waited. Maybe he needed it as much as I did. At least, I like to think so. I wallowed in the memories all night and by the time the sun crested the horizon, I was dressed my meager belongings packed.

Only David and my aunt were present to see me off. I waited patiently for my ride. Like the night before, time slowed to a crawl; a prisoner in a world in which I no longer had a place.

Gary, a social worker, finally arrived. I waited for a hug from my aunt, but it never came, and David squirmed as I gave him what I figured was our last hug.

Oconto, a small town, forty-five miles north of Green Bay, was to be my new home. As I walked toward Gary's car, I wondered for the thousandth time what I'd ever done to cause my extended family to hate me; to want me gone from their lives. I often wondered if I had been allowed to talk to Kathy, if things would have been different.

Psychologically, society tried to force me to forget; to pretend it didn't happen that my world had not been turned upside down. So, I buried it. Deep down where I didn't have to deal with it. And that was fine with me.

On March 5, 1976, my aunt and uncle terminated their guardianship and placed both David and I with the state of Wisconsin. The Juvenile records of that termination plainly states that no other family member was willing to accept the responsibility of two orphaned children.

Maslow's Hierarchy of needs diminished down to one; my physiological needs were met. I no longer felt safe; I had fear infesting the corners of my mind. I had no sense of belonging; opposing to receiving or giving love. My self-esteem and self-actualization diminished, I stopped playing the piano and tucked away my creative talents.

According to Richardson (1995), when dealing with differences after the unexpected happens; there is the 'cut-off'; the only way to deal with such tragedy is to withdraw either physically or emotionally when things get too tense for them. I feel my relatives and the court system did the best they knew how; they all felt powerless and by doing the cut-off that were their immediate way out.

Adolescence (13-19 years) contiuned…

What is unique about the stage of Identity is that it is a special sort of synthesis of earlier stages and a special sort of anticipation of later ones. Youth is a time of radical change—the great body changes accompanying puberty, the ability of the mind to search one's own intentions and the intentions of others, the suddenly sharpened awareness of the roles society has offered for later life.

Adolescents "are confronted by the need to re-establish [boundaries] for themselves and to do this in the face of an often potentially hostile world." At this point, one is in a state of 'identity confusion', but society normally makes allowances for youth to "find themselves," and this state is called the moratorium.

Chapter 6
Kathy, a beautiful flower

~Truly, I was surprised to see such a strange creature called a Praying Mantis climbing up my arm. Kathy reassured me that it wouldn't harm me and most of all that it was a creation from God.~

My older sister, Kathy was not told of the accident for six days. Unaware, she didn't attend the funeral, missing the only opportunity she had to say goodbye.

Kathy, the rebellious teenager, was now twenty-one years old. Although she liked the hippie life, protesting and free love, she was still our sister. Her running away from home whenever she got the chance, wasn't because of drugs, she simply wanted to go her own way. It hurt our parents and I'm sure they wondered more than once where they'd gone wrong.

The more Kathy was away, the more I missed her. When she was home, she, more than anyone, made me feel special and loved. She was my rock and took me for walks in the woods and pointed out interesting insects and pretty leaves. It was a magical for just the two of us. I always thought that whatever had gone wrong in my life, Kathy could fix it.

Like me, Kathy suffered the tragedy the best way she knew how, and I wanted to give her the opportunity to tell her story in our own words and how she tried to keep us altogether...

I was staying with my friend Holly and her husband, in Madison, Wisconsin, three and a half hours from home. I felt good that

A Family's Fairytale Turned Upside Down

warm, summer day and just like in the movies, the ringing of a phone shattered my entire life.

Holly answered the phone and I knew immediately something was wrong. When she hung up, her hands were shaking and she could barely speak. Finally, she asked me to drive into town with her. Believing something was wrong to actually knowing, kept my questions at bay. I couldn't make myself ask.

Once in town, we went to a restaurant, chose a table by the windows, and waited. Holly asked what I wanted to drink and what kind of cigarettes I wanted. That's when I knew the "something wrong" involved me. Holly already knew those answers.

Two cars raced into the parking lot and my heart sank. It was Sue, a friend and Gayle, my foster sister. Immediately, I thought of my boyfriend, Barry. Screaming at Holly, I begged her to tell me what had happened to him.

Sue came up to me, put her hand on my shoulder, and said, "Kathy, it's not Barry." She took a deep breath and delivered the worst news a young woman could ever hear. "There's been an accident, honey. I'm sorry, but your mom, dad, Kim and your other sister, her name starts with an M, I can't remember which, they—they all died. Kathy, I'm so sorry."

I don't remember much of what happened after that. Shock, grief, fear—it all rained down around me like Niagara Falls. I do remember I wondered if it had been Melissa who died. Even though I loved all my siblings, Missy, as I called her, was very special to me. There was a bond and I remember crying at the thought—please don't let it be Missy. Then I sobbed, because Monica was just as precious, but not as close to me. Guilt for wanting one sister over the other haunted me. From that point until I saw Melissa, was a blur of anguish and despair.

Because of my lifestyle, my aunts and uncles prevented me from seeing Missy, Russell, and David. They were convinced I would hurt them. These were my brothers and sister—I'd die before hurting any of them. My aunt, during one phone conversation said, "You killed your parents a long time ago." How is that for a crap load of guilt to burden a young woman? My only concern was for my younger siblings and I wanted to keep what was left of the family together. Tragedies have a way of making a person grow up fast and even though I had doubts as to whether I could do it or not, I still wanted the opportunity to try.

Finally, at the end of June, I was permitted a brief visit with Missy. Tears coursing down her face, the first thing she said to me was, "Kathy, they threw all our toys away."

My heart splintered into a thousand pieces, and to this day, I'm not sure all the slivers have been mended. I wanted more than anything to take my remaining siblings, set up housekeeping in our own home and raise them in the place they'd known love and safety.

Again, because of my hippie ways, protesting Viet Nam and father's rights, I was a bad seed. At this point, I had dabbled with drugs, but hadn't liked any of them and stayed away from them. Yet, my aunts and uncles refused my pleas to take the children and make a home for them. I went so far as to talk to an attorney, but because the aunt and uncle had the GAL, the attorney informed me the legal battle could take years. I didn't have the money or know-how to continue that fight. And because they termed me a bum, a hippie, and drug addict—not fit to raise a child—much less three, the attorney didn't hold out much hope. Nor did my past help, either. As he so plainly worded it, "If you ran away from home when things were good, how could anyone expect you to stick around and take care of three kids?"

I did get a co-executor at the bank where my parents did business, to help me stop the aunts and uncles from raping our home.

Money that should have come to us was used to pay those same relatives on renovations to a house that didn't need extensive work.

My visits to Missy, Russell, and David were limited, and I was told they needed a clean break. A clean break *from a sister who loved them?* A clean break *from being together?*

At the reading of the will, I went up to my uncle to give him a hug. Just a simple showing of affection, but my aunt knocked my hands away and said, "No. Grow up. Get over it."

Oh, yeah, I was going to go back to my wild life and pretend none of this happened and bury the guilt that I had failed my brothers and sister. How could anyone ever get over that?

In 1977, three years after the accident, I talked to the man who had hit my parent's car. We talked on the phone to start, then we went to dinner. I just wanted to see the man who had caused such heartache and pain. But looking at him, I couldn't hold on to hate or resentment. Unfortunately, his punishment for four deaths will forever remain a mystery to me. He received nine months in the county jail and a two year suspension on his driver's license. My entire family's lives were destroyed in one way or the other and this man simply walked away with little consequence. Justice? Not by a long shot. After a long soul-search, I realized it wouldn't do me or my family any good to hold on to those resentments and hatred. I forgave him.

At twenty-one, I lost my entire family, through death and ignorance, my self-respect and dignity. From that, my life spiraled out of control. If my family thought I was no good, then it must be true.

Kathy did what she could to keep us together. But even at twenty-one, Kathy didn't realized she could have fought those aunts and uncles and possibly have won. They were so adamant in their belief of Kathy's radical, drug-filled lifestyle, she felt she had no avenues left open to her.

Although she had protested for other people's right—it was her own that she should have protested the most.

Chapter 7
Losing Myself to the World

~Moments pass and I cannot be found. How do I cope with my pain? Who is she, where is she, and will she be back?~

It was time to make my own way in the world. As I made that trip to Oconto, I left everything I'd known behind and was headed down a tunnel to hell. Few words were spoken on that trip and I remember staring out the window, wondering where I was going and how bad it would be.

The radio played softly in the background and *Dream Weaver* by Gary Wright came on. It soothed me somewhat, but worry and fear about this place I was going kept me tense and on edge. Krueger Receiving Home in Oconto, Wisconsin. It was a transition home where I was to be evaluated and find the best fit for a foster home.

I knew other kids my age would be there, but what kind of kids? Would I find friends there, or would they all shun me? Before I was ready, we pulled up in front of a large family-style home. It looked friendly from the outside, but I knew from experience that what showed on the outside wasn't necessarily how it really was on the inside.

Getting settled, I didn't say much, but watched what was happening around me, the kids that passed me in the hallways and how they reacted. This would be the first time in my life I would spend a night away from home in a strange house.

I made one friend there. Her name was Robin. She was my age, but more adventurous. She convinced me to go on a date with two guys we'd just met and although apprehensive, I agreed. Robin knew the streets and I clung to her, drinking my first beer that night. Bad decisions have a way of coming back to bite you and that night was no exception. I got drunk and one of the boys raped me in a cold, dark pick-up bed. I don't remember his face, don't remember him even kissing me, but I do remember feeling that it was just one more indignity to live through. I no longer had anyone to talk to, to help me make good decisions, and to be concerned about my well-being. I was lost in a sea of pain, both physically and emotionally and somehow it just didn't matter. The dawning of the day was cold as the boys dropped us off in front of the receiving home. Robin stayed with them, but I was dumped off like unwanted garbage and I felt as though that's exactly what I was. Garbage to be dumped when no longer useful.

    I did admire Robin's courage and strength, but after that night, I didn't go with her anymore. I'd see her curly red hair bouncing and her freckled face smiling as she drove away with those same two boys. I felt dirty and unwanted. Four months later, I left the home and never saw her again, but I do hope Robin found what she was looking for.

    One evening on a beautiful spring day, I was sitting at the dining room table when the phone rang. It was my cousin who called to say that David would be adopted by a family in Sturgeon Bay. I hung up, conflicting emotions raging through my body. I was happy that David would have a family, but hopes that we would one day be together again flared in a burst of flames, killing that fantasy.

    I tried keeping in touch with him, wrote to him often, (through his adoptive mother) but rarely received a reply.

When I did, it was generic in nature and told me almost nothing about my little brother. When I heard the details had been finalized, I lost that tiny spark of hope that what was left of my family would eventually get back together. Because of the court's idea of what was best for us, they kept contact between us at a minimum so we could have consistency in our lives. I didn't need consistency, I needed my family.

At school, I would leave a notebook on the lunchroom table on purpose. A notebook I had filled with lies, hoping someone would find it and think I was cool enough to have as a friend. I lied about smoking, drugs, sex, whatever popped into my mind, I wrote about it in my notebook. But since I was from the Receiving Home, I was a bad person, someone to avoid so the bad luck that got me there wouldn't rub off on the "normal" kids. Because to them, I wasn't normal—I was someone to ignore, a non-entity.

One good thing did come from that school. I joined the gymnastics' team and found I was good at it. Like my perfect footsteps, the balance beam became my stability. If I could master it, turn my somersault with perfection and land with style and grace, then I was important. I mattered. Even if no one else thought so, it meant something to me.

Even though suicide didn't enter my mind, I lived in a state of depression twenty-four hours a day. I hated waking up each morning, knowing it was another day alone. I had a small cut on my thigh from the accident and to make sure I was still alive, I'd inflict pain over the cut by highlighting with a red ink pen, which, of course, made it look worse. My small scar was nothing compared to my brothers or the death that rained down on my family that evening, but it was a way to acknowledge that I had not gotten off scott free. I *was* hurt and this scar was a reminder of that.

I attended my first school dance and don't remember if I danced with a boy or not, but one boy in my Homeroom class had a crush on me, but told me I needed to lose weight. Then he'd be my boyfriend. It was another confirmation that I was not good enough, that I had to be different to be loved and accepted.

The courts were in the process of finding a home for me. When asked if I wanted to live in the country or city, I said city. It seemed to me that if I lived within walking distance of other families, I would find friends that might help me through these miserable years.

Of course, they didn't listen and I went to live forty-five miles north of Green Bay in the middle of nowhere. Another disappointment to live with, but I had no control and my wishes were ignored—again. Even my visitation with Kathy and my brothers were supervised. I was never allowed to be alone with them, never able to talk about what was happening in our lives or talk about the pain of losing so many members at once. Because we couldn't be ourselves and talk about what was on our mind, we grew further apart.

At sixteen and three foster homes and four high schools later, I ended up in Oconto Falls. I was sixteen. My foster family wanted to adopt me, but I refused. I had lost everything that fateful June day and I would be damned if I would lose my name—my identity as well. It was my one and only link to the family I had lost.

The foster family, both teachers with small children and one on the way, felt fake from the very beginning. As the days wore on, I became nothing more than a glorified babysitter. Since my foster dad taught at the school I attended, I felt I had no privacy whatsoever. My depression, fear, anxiety all made itself known as I learned words I had no business using and inflicted their horribleness on my teachers. They, of course, went to my foster dad for advice on how to handle discipline and how to stop my rebellion. I was expelled and suspended. And that suited me fine. I didn't have to go to school, didn't have to deal with the teachers or the kids, I got to sleep in and do what I wanted to do. Some punishment. And it didn't help. I continued to be a smart mouth—said whatever came to mind at the moment.

I was bullied because of my checkered path. No one really knew what to believe about me and because my foster dad was a teacher, it was really bad. Every dig, every snub cut away my identity and I acted out just so people would know that I was alive—that I mattered, even if in a bad way.

Rumors in school flew about how my family died. Someone thought they had died in a fire and asked, "What degree burns did you get?"

I lashed out, "So many you can't see them or are you blind?" I let them know how it really happened, but it was like I was diseased and no one wanted anything to do with me.

Christmas that first year at my foster home sucked. I remembered the fun we used to have when we'd spend Christmas Eve at Grandma's house along with our other relatives—yes, the same ones that sent us all away—and how there were always plenty of good food, laughter and teasing.

At midnight, we'd head off to Mass, Staying awake that late was hard at times, but once we hit the cold night air, I would wake up fast. One particular Christmas the priest announced that a family had lost everything in a fire. Thankfully, they had all survived, but their possessions, Christmas presents—everything was gone. He asked if anyone could donate to this family, it would be much appreciated.

Dad talked to us about donating the presents we had gotten from Grandma to these people and we all agreed. That was the way Dad was. He taught me about love we should share unconditionally and giving with the right hand while not questioning the left hand.

At home, the joyous sounds of Burl Ives, Bing Crosby and others filled the house along with the wonderful smells of baking. What a wonderful way to wake up in the morning.

As I watched my foster father try to be a dad to me, I rejected him as I remembered my real dad. We spent a lot of time at my grandparent's house. They lived by the bay and we had a lot of exciting things to do—collecting rocks, fishing for catfish or yellow-bellied bullheads. Dad spent a lot of time with his parents knowing he wouldn't have them much longer. And he'd been right. They were both gone by the time we'd had the accident. But I'll never forget how much we loved them and the fun we had when we visited.

Dad volunteered to help build St. Francis church and St. Mary's as well. It was something he felt he needed to do, to give back to the community and for himself as well.

At the foster home, Christmas seemed so commercial, so generic. It was all about the presents, not helping those in need and with just a few people at the house on Christmas Eve, I missed our large, noisy family gathering.

A Family's Fairytale Turned Upside Down

On Sunday, after church, we went our separate ways, and I couldn't help compare this reality to the one where Dad would come home from church and gather us kids for a game of Bocce Ball, badminton, croquet or basketball. If the games got too rowdy, someone usually got hurt, but we still had a good time and Sunday afternoons was when I missed my dad the most.

During the summer of 1977, I got a job at Round Roof Restaurant. I was seventeen. My job was bussing tables. That was my first look at a regular bar. I remember glancing inside the darkened room, hearing laughter and loud chatter. People were having a good time. The smell of stale beer wafted out the doors and I wanted so badly to be a part of that friendly scene.

While at work, my existence was noted, even if only to tell me to get the tables cleaned off a little faster, but I felt like someone actually noticed me. But when my foster dad would come to pick me up after my shift, I wasn't the cool chick I had envisioned in my mind. I was the loser—the girl who had nothing or no one.

My foster parents refused to let me get a job the following year, saying I needed to concentrate on being a kid. I've often thought of their reasoning behind that decision. Maybe they were trying, in their own way to shield me, to help me come to terms with my situation or maybe they just wanted to close to home so they didn't have to make that extra effort to run me to work and back. I'll never know. I do know, I wanted to stand up and scream at them that my family was dead, but I wasn't. I was standing right in front of them. See ME not what I represented—a child of tragedy. I resented it and them, especially when my teacher dad refused to let me take the senior skip day like all the others. Instead, they said I had to come home, there was work to be done and the punishment for "skipping" would be severe.

The thought of driving myself back and forth to work, filled me with dread. What if another drunk driver finished the job the first one started? At that point, I wasn't sure it mattered if I died or not, but a deep-seated fear wouldn't let me try. It wasn't until I was eighteen that I became brave enough to get my driver's license.

And then I discovered their liquor cabinet. I would wait until they had gone somewhere, pour myself a drink and pretend I was in the Round Roof Restaurant bar, having a good time with my "friends." So they wouldn't notice the dwindling booze supply, I'd add water to bring the level back up to where it was.

I remember attending a party one time and I woke up in the bathtub, vomit all over me, with not a clue how I had gotten there. This party, I had thought, would be my saving grace. Go to the party, drink a little to fit in and make friends. It didn't happen that way and I was grounded for weeks for it.

Days and months passed as I struggled through the years, fighting the depression, loneliness and despair. Off and on, I tried to contact Kathy through the mail, by phone and by asking people if they knew where she was. She'd been told so often that she needed to stay out of our lives, that she had pretty much cut off all contact. What little time we did have together was strained. We'd been away from each other too long to be able to react well together. The accident and treatment of family during the aftermath was painful to discuss and was quietly and bitterly ignored.

My graduation day was fast approaching. During my senior year, I met Mark, a man seven years older than me. I supposed I looked at him like a father figure, which wasn't a good call on my part, but he professed to love me and I'd been aching for that kind of love for a long time. It was a new beginning, a big event and each time my life changed, that's the way I looked at it. A new start. Sometimes it was good, sometimes it wasn't.

I graduated in the spring of 1978. To me it was just another day as my family wasn't there to celebrate with me. I finally understood Pinocchio; all he wanted was to be a real boy and have a real family to call his own. I wanted the same thing because I had repressed so many feelings over the years, I felt as I was just a wooden girl going through the motions of life.

On June 14th, I turned eighteen and left my foster home to spread my wings. I moved out that day, finally able to make my own decisions, right or wrong, and to hopefully find the love I so desperately needed.

At dinner that night, Mark proposed to me on bended knee, holding a gorgeous ring in one hand. I was shocked, but accepted. What else was I supposed to do? I wanted protection and security as well as love and he could provide all my needs.

I said yes for all the wrong reasons. And while I had no self-esteem or self-worth, I still chose badly. I was vulnerable and needy and he was looking for someone to control.

I moved in with him and our first night as lovers left a lot to be desired, but having experienced a rape when I was fifteen, I didn't know any different. Still, I thought I had found my "home," my one true place to be.

That summer, I tried to be as good a partner as I could, tried to be just like my mother, but I didn't understand how things were supposed to work and how Mom accomplished everything she did on a daily basis.

This was also the year that my inheritance was waiting for me.

Maslow's Hierarchy of needs started to build up for the first time since the accident. My physiological needs were fulfilled. I felt safe from harm, and I had no fear that my relationship with Mark was good. I felt like I belonged and loved Mark and his family and friends. I had no self-esteem and self actualization. I clung to Mark and his ways of life, not knowing my next steps to take to go forward in life. I trusted Mark that he would provide for me a healthy and safe environment.

McMahan (2009): girl's growth spurts start at about ten and for boys, approximately around the age of twelve. As McMahan reported, "The growth spurt in adolescence does not go smoothly and evenly."

Melissa Woitula-Alberts

Missy and David

Missy, Kim, David, Monica, Russell

David

Russell, Missy, Kim, Monica and Kathy

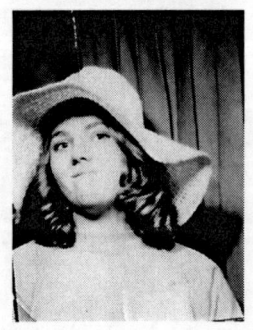

Missy

Missy's 1st Communion

A Family's Fairytale Turned Upside Down

Joe Woitula. Jr.

Missy and Monica

Peggy Woitula

Missy, Kathy and baby Erin

Russell

Woitula car at accident site

~I have overcome many obstacles while the devil had many chances to destroy me. I believe God put a halt to the pain and suffering that had followed me throughout the years. Once I had nothing, then I began to trust and held on to my faith. Now I grip tightly onto hope, grace and the many promises that will follow. "Boom."~

Chapter 8
How Deep Can I Go?

~The reoccurring pain is bottomless with never-ending torture of my past. If I dig deep enough, maybe I will be forgotten too.~

When it came time to claim my inheritance, Mark's mother took me to the Green Bay attorney and bank to settle up. I had suggested Kathy be present, but was told that she was nothing but trouble and they didn't want her involved. Again, they wanted to sever the relationship with my surviving family, to pretend they no longer existed either.

I had just turned eighteen and was feeling good about making my own decisions, but realized I still I had no control over my life. I had lost so much and they (the courts and adults in my life) knew Kathy was the only sister I had left, but still they continued to advise to me stay away from her. I wanted acceptance from the adults that surrounded me, but I also wanted Kathy.

My inheritance quickly went in one pocket and out the other. I was too immature to realize it needed to be invested or saved. At eighteen, all I could see were dollar signs. And it was blood money. I just wanted to be rid of it as fast as I could. Every dollar reminded me of why I had it in the first place and I didn't want it around any longer than necessary. I paid cash for almost everything, even buying a seven thousand dollar car.

My relationship with Mark was okay, although he made it plain he didn't want me to have anything to do with my family either. He wanted to control, to isolate me, to have him for himself. That wasn't the way I saw my life going and my resentment grew.

He worked hard for everything he had and the bills were paid on time and he had goals, but that wasn't enough to satisfy the hole I had in my heart.

It was the height of the disco era and I wanted to dance. My wings were strained with the necessity of holding them close to me when they wanted to soar. Music and the nightlife enticed me and I spent a lot of time in small country bars, but I wanted the flavor of the big discotheques in the city. I wanted to party and dance until the last song played.

In spite of the notebook that said I did, I didn't smoke or do drugs, but alcohol became my drug of choice, quickly becoming an alcoholic. The liquor released my inhibitions and I reveled in it.

Shopping was also an addiction and I bought disco clothes and shoes or whatever struck my fancy. Back home after one foray in Green Bay, Mark met me at the door, grabbing my purchases from me. One by one, he took them out of the bags and threw them against the wall.

As the shampoo flew through the air, he yelled, "Isn't shopping in Oconto Falls good enough for you?"

I wasn't quite ready for the relationship to melt down, and I decided he was probably right. I settled for living in a small town in the country, trying to convince myself that was all I needed.

But it wasn't. And deep down, I knew it. I began to dress up as though going to the disco and drink myself silly. My heart had shattered; I was in pain and wanted everyone around me to hurt as badly as I did.

A Family's Fairytale Turned Upside Down

What I had thought to be a decent, if not, wonderful relationship, deteriorated and the abuse came swiftly when I did something to displease him. Both physically and sexually, I suffered through the abuse, believing him as he'd yell, "You're worthless and no one else would want you."

I attended a local technical college, taking clerical classes, but unsatisfied and unsure where my life was going, I quit school and used some of my money to visit my aunt and uncle in Arizona. It was a bittersweet visit, remembering the trips we made in that baby blue station wagon and I couldn't imagine how my parents managed with five kids on such a long journey.

I found the unconditional love in Arizona from an aunt and uncle that had had no part in the fiasco that happened at home when my parents died. This acceptance and love had eluded me in Wisconsin, yet I knew I couldn't stay in Arizona. However bad Wisconsin was, it was my home, the only place I knew and Mark was there. I had to go back. But for those few precious months, I felt that specialness that I had been searching for.

When I returned home, he had taken over the farm from his retired parents. I thought having a farm with land and animals would be good for me, but I had already had a taste of freedom and I liked it. So, I used more of the money I didn't want and went on a Caribbean Cruise. Mark was livid, but that taste of freedom had been so wonderful, I wanted more. When I returned, I knew being his partner was the last thing I wanted.

After my return home, the stress of dealing with a farm on a daily basis brought out a mean streak in Mark. He drank a lot and I know my free spirit didn't help the situation any. Things got worse instead of better and I loathed where I was in my life and wanted out. The farm I had so looked forward to didn't help.

I hated the farm work. Milking every morning and night was way beyond my capacity, but I felt I was being molded into someone I didn't want to be. I gained weight, which I hated, dyed my hair blonde thinking it would make a difference. But nothing changed.

One cold December night Mark asked me to help get the cows in the barn to be milked. I tried but the mud and manure was deep and I began to cry as he screamed at me to move it.

When the last cow was in the pen, he threw me into a pen with a bull and tried to spook the animal. I was so scared I started crying. He laughed, called me a baby and finally let me out.

I wanted out—out of the farm work and out of the relationship. I sought out a local church for guidance, but when I got home, he slapped me and told me I was a bad person for going to church. In terror, I went to a place in my mind he couldn't reach, but I knew it was only a matter of time before he hurt me beyond repair.

While I cried, I thought about my mother and the emotional breakdown she'd had a few years before the accident. Dad took her to a mental health facility to recuperate while us kids went to stay with family and friends. Dad had to work and couldn't take the time off to stay with us. I wondered what had caused her breakdown, but I knew if I didn't get out of here, I'd be facing the same thing.

In anger, I would threaten to leave, but he swore he'd break my legs and that I was nothing I could do about it. I was a whore, good for nothing and nobody cared anything about me. When told something on a daily basis, it becomes a truth, at least it did in my mind and I felt I had no place to go, that I would never find what I so desperately needed—someone to love me for who I was, not who they tried to make me become.

The following December, I got up my nerve, packing a small suitcase of personal items and clothing and hid them in a snow bank beside the house. When he fell asleep, I wrote him a note saying I would be back the next day for the rest of my stuff and I would be bringing the police with me. I placed the engagement ring on the note and went to a girlfriend's house. I barely slept the rest of the night, worrying about what kind of reception I would get the next day—cops or not.

When we arrived, he was on the couch, curled up in a ball, crying, "Don't leave me, oh, please don't leave me."

Looking at him, I knew it was finally over. "One person," I said, "can take just so much and then it's time I move on."

For the first time since the accident, I felt good about my future.

Maslow's Hierarchy of needs diminished down to nothing. After leaving Mark, I was homeless; but having none of the physiological needs being met, I was okay with that because I was out of an abusive relationship. The only safety I had was my blood money and my car. I had no sense of belonging or commitment of love to anyone or anything and definitely no self-esteem or self-actualization

Chapter 9
Disco in 60 Minutes

~When the sun set; life rose within my soul. I hide in the daylight my flesh to live the night life. I believed I was a bursting star in the galaxy called "Missy." How long is an hour? Sometimes a lifetime.~

Life was finally about me. No one else—just me. I was ready for the spotlight and to make people notice me. I was on top of the world and confident enough to soar.

The city offered a variety of bars and dance clubs and I hit them all. My favorite was Jungle Fever, where I would dance all night. It seemed, for a time, to fill the emptiness inside me and I carried it to the extreme. Dancing for attention became my goal every night.

I moved back to my hometown, thinking I would find satisfaction and acceptance, but again was disappointed. I did get a small apartment, a few things to fill it and for the first time in a long time, I had no boundaries at all and it felt good.

It was a girl's night out at Jungle Fever and Happy Hour. I finally got up the nerve to try a vodka gimlet. It didn't take long for it to take effect as I wasn't used to drinking that much. As I kept drinking, I spotted a dancers pole in the corner, a mirror behind it smudged with fingerprints. I got up and walked over to it, self-consciousness fled and I began to dance, my hands sliding down the silvery slickness as manufactured smoke swirled around my ankles. As I danced, I noticed people watching me and my movements became more and more sexual. I was being accepted—I was being applauded and cheered. It was pure ecstasy and I gave it all I had, so lost in the fact that these people were cheering for me, that I was the center of attention. It was like a sexual awakening. The ego boost was beyond anything I have ever experienced and I loved it.

I partied all night and slept all day. My past became a handicap I couldn't escape. I continued searching for ways to fill a void in my soul, but it just got bigger and bigger. Don Williams sang it best "looking for love in all the wrong places," should have been my theme song. My choices were downright silly. It was as though I had forgotten had to love.

In time, the nightlife began to bore me. It was the same old crowd and the same old lines as men tried to woo me into their beds. It finally dawned on me that I was using sex to take the place of love and I felt dirty and cheap.

I was looking for myself and had no idea where or who I was. I started and quit college several times, took jobs that I knew I wouldn't like, but did it anyway in the hopes that something would spark—that I would find where I was supposed to be in life. It didn't happen. Nothing had staying power and I was footloose and rambling without any direction and no one to help me find what I searched for so desperately.

As much as I wanted my family back, I didn't bother trying to find Russell or David or even Kathy, who I looked up to and adored. It was as though I simply stopped caring and lost interest.

My life became about *me*. What I wanted, what I felt and I didn't care if I hurt people along the way. I figured if I hurt them first, they wouldn't have the chance to hurt me and the hurting game went both ways. I didn't have a purpose, didn't care. By the time I turned twenty, I was burnt out, used up and just as lonely as I'd ever been. Ragged and torn inside, my pain knew no bounds.

Finally, I did try to contact my relatives. As soon as they heard my voice it was as though they shut down, and I could tell they didn't want to talk to me. Maybe it was guilt from what they'd done, or not done, maybe it was my imagination, but the rebuff was there and it hurt all over again.

It seemed as if I couldn't commit to anything, even college. If I didn't like a teacher or a class, I'd walk out and do something else. I couldn't seem to settle into anything for any length of time.

Selfish choices were the norm. I didn't care what others thought, didn't care how they treated me. It was all bull anyway and sooner or later someone would prove I wasn't wrong about my attitude, about people just waiting to stick the knife in when my back was turned.

I shied away from of my girlfriends because they'd talk about their parent's. One girl said, "Mom and Dad went to Florida for two weeks and I was lost, because I wasn't able to talk to Mom several times a day."

It was all said in innocence, she didn't mean any harm, but I wanted to scream at her that I hadn't been able to speak to my mother for six years. It would have been nice to be able to pick up the phone and call Mom for advice, to go by and see her to just visit and let her help me make the right decisions. But I had no one to do that. I was on my own and it wasn't what I thought it would be.

A Family's Fairytale Turned Upside Down

Mother's Day was awful. Father's Day was always cold and dark, even if the sun was shining. Every year, Mother's Day remained the hardest for me to get through and for many years filled my heart with such loneliness I could hardly breathe.

Eventually, I did try to reconnect with my brothers and sister, but we had drifted apart emotionally and had our own lives to live. We simply didn't know how to be a family after all that time.

I kept in touch with David through his adoptive mother, but one day, I received this letter from her:

Dear Missy,

Received Dave's letter yesterday and we talked about it between all of us. I told him I have been writing to you and he asked if I would continue to do this. He said he would add to it if he felt like writing. We all need to remember Dave is only eleven and a half and still has a lot of growing to do. Do you remember when you were eleven? Missy, you are an adult, thinking like an adult, Dave is still a child. After visiting family services for eighteen months—we found out that he needs to have a childhood. He loves you and thinks about you but that's all I can say. He really doesn't like talking about it. So please understand how he feels. I know you can understand and know where he is coming from and hopefully where he should go. But he's the one to decide but with our love and prayers and the support of all his needs he will be able to do it. Well I have to go to work.

All our prayers and love,

I didn't try to contact him very much after that. He didn't respond most of the time and I felt his mother was telling me to back off. David had been in our family such a short time that I doubted he even remembered Mom and Dad anymore. Maybe he did, but the pain of being ignored was too much for me.

    I held on to the dark emotions swirling through my mind because any feeling was better than nothing at all. My depression deepened and I felt I had nothing much to live for. And I had no place to go. No safety net waiting for me anywhere.

Chapter 10
Mysteries of Amore

~Loss of a loved one is painful. You have them on your mind, they are the last thing you think of before going to sleep and the first thing you think of in the morning~

No safety net didn't stop me from looking for that special someone. But the dates I went on turned into nightmares and I stopped trying so hard.

Then, at a party one night, I met George. Immediately, I knew he was my Knight in Shining Armor. Tall, dark and handsome, just my type. When he heard my last name, he was shocked and told me that his friend had been at the accident that night and told him about it.

It seemed to bond us closer together. However, George carried baggage of his own, having been married and had two sons. When I met him, he was in the process of getting a divorce and I hesitated to start a relationship with him for some time.

Finally, we moved in together and I knew it was right. I told him of my sordid past. Loving and caring, he suggested that since Memorial Day was coming up, we go to the gravesites; that it might be good for me.

I refused. I wanted to remember my family as they were, not buried in the cold ground. He didn't push the issue, but one day I had told him of living on Tulip Street and that red tulips were my mom's favorite flower. He surprised me with red tulips and said we should plant them. For the first time since the accident, I felt like someone actually listened to me. We planted them on Memorial Day.

Neither of us was over-eager to get back into a serious relationship. Both of our first relationships had not turned out well and we were not going to jump back into it easily. But we talked. And talked. At times it was as if the whole world disappeared and George and I were the only ones left. For the first time since the accident, I began to open my heart to someone and could actually see a future in front of me.

In 1982, I entered college in Wisconsin and was asked by Julie, a girl in the cafeteria to go to a Christian coffeehouse. I didn't hang out with Christian people. The thought of letting some stranger or better yet, an invisible God into my life just didn't set well within my soul. But George and I did attend and I realized it was the first Friday night in a long time that I was not at a bar.

Planning the wedding, seeing my friends and a few relatives filled my heart. It was also a sad day because it would be Russell giving me away instead of my father. Kathy, with whom I had been seeing more often, was my Maid of Honor. When the ceremony was over, I turned around and there stood George's mother, all dressed up, a corsage pinned to her lapel and a big smile on her face. On the bride's side, was the heart-breaking vision of four empty chairs in the front row and I could almost see my own mother there, tears of joy streaming down her face. Oh, if it were only true.

My relationship with Kathy, at this time, had gotten better and we saw each other occasionally. On October 1, 1983, with Kathy as Maid of Honor and Russell giving me away, George and I were married under a neighbor's willow tree. To this day, I still have the branch he made into a simple wreath from that wonderful tree. And to this day, George and I are still together.

George's sons, Shawn and Shane became "my" sons as well and I loved them with all my heart. As a newlywed, I began to feel a purpose in my life. I was wanted for the first time in a very long time. I assured them I was not there to replace their mother and we developed a wonderful relationship.

George and I vowed we would stay celibate for a minimum of two weeks. It was hard, but we accomplished it. It was something we felt we needed to do, a way of cleansing, I suppose. But it was the right decision and I wished many times that I had not had the sexual experiences I had had previously so I could have went into this marriage bed with no knowledge of what sex was really like.

I had done my share of partying, met some strange people along the way, but I now saw a way of life that other people had shared with me; that of Christianity. At that time in my life, they were some of the strange people I met along the way. But some had had a peace about them that I had yet to find. George and I were trying hard to turn our lives around; to make a good life for us.

We began attending a Free Methodist church in Green Bay. All the words spoken during the services seemed foreign to me, but I wanted to know more. We purchased a Bible and started attending Bible classes. The God that I was hearing about entered my heart, mysterious and almost more than I could grasp.

As we continued going to church and church camps, the bitterness I had harbored for so many years began to fade away. There was something greater out there and I meant to find it.

At Sky Lodge Christian Camp in Montello, Wisconsin, was our first family vacation. One evening there was an altar call while the song, *I am the Potter and You Are the Clay* played George, Shawn, Shane and myself walked to the altar and gave our lives to God.

We knew from that moment on there was a God and He was bigger than anything we'd ever known. Although I had given my life to God, I still held back. Too many years of not being able to trust was hard for me to let go. Independent to a fault, I wanted what I wanted, not what God wanted for me.

At times I resented George because he still had a family and couldn't possibly know how I felt. And sometimes I wanted him to know the pain I had been in since I was thirteen years old.

George's mother had diabetes and one evening he got a phone call that she was in the hospital. The doctor said it was serious and that in the next few weeks, it was possible she could lose both legs.

When he got off the phone, he hugged me tightly, crying like a baby that his mother would have to go through that and could die. He apologized to me for not comprehending my hurt and that he'd never realized how empty I must have felt all those years living with a Mother and all she had to offer. We bonded even more over this revelation and we began to start our own traditions.

Thanksgiving was our first holiday together. George, Shawn, Shane and I spent hours making homemade pilgrims and turkeys and we beat Indian drums made from Quaker oat containers.

As we made new memories, I remembered old ones. Dad watching the parade and football games. Me helping Mom with the holiday preparations. I remember the elegantly decorated apron she would drape around my neck as we mixed, chopped and cooked. Mom always wore her black pumps with a skirt and blouse, her smile delightful with her ruby red lipstick. My main job was to set the table with the finest linen we owned, offset by beautiful dishes and candles.

It was a tradition that we would hold hands, say grace and then one by one around the table, each person had an opportunity to say what they were thankful for. It was touching to hear, especially when Mom or Dad would thank God for having such a wonderful family. I sat and smiled.

Now, their memories were pleasant and I could smile as I re-lived those days in my mind. It was the first time since I'd lost them that I could think of them without the bitterness clogging my heart.

Maslow's Hierarchy of needs began to build up. My physiological needs were met. I felt safe and secure in my home and I had no fear because George was now my protector and I trusted him. My sense of belonging came forth, I was now a wife to a man that I could be friends with. The love and acceptance from Shawn and Shane boosted my sense of belonging. Together George and I had a nice network of friends.

Erikson's Early Adulthood (20-40 years) Love: Intimacy vs. Isolation (Young adulthood, 20-24, or 20-40 years)

- **Existential Question: Can I Love?**

The Intimacy vs. Isolation conflict is emphasized around the age of 30. Young adults are still eager to blend their identities with friends. They want to fit in. Erikson also argues that "Intimacy has a counterpart: Distantiation: the readiness to isolate and if necessary, to destroy those forces and people whose essence seems dangerous to our own, and whose territory seems to encroach on the extent of one's intimate relations." (1950)

Once people have established their identities, they are ready to make long-term commitments to others. They become capable of forming intimate, reciprocal relationships and willingly make the sacrifices and compromises that such relationships require. If people cannot form these intimate relationships – perhaps because of their own needs—a sense of isolation may result.

Chapter 11
Unconditional Love

~Many times we cannot see the goodness in what life brings our way for it takes time. When the harvest is ripe both inside and out, then and only then are we ready. Just like different seasons of our lives, it too, can be turned over and the finest results will show in the end~

I was pregnant. It brought me to a new level of responsibility and I refused to put anything harmful into my system. When the nurse asked me about my immunization records, my eyes welled with tears and I told her I didn't know if I'd had mumps, measles or chicken pox.

Titer tests were required. Her question ate at me and I realized I didn't know a thing about my family's health. That information had perished with my parents. I wondered if Mom's pregnancies were easy or hard. I remembered David being born, but sharing that kind of information with a young child was not done in those days. I just knew she went to the hospital and came home with David.

It was hard dealing with a new baby with no one to turn to for advice. George's mother helped where she could, but her health prevented her from being with me when Sarah was sick or in pain and I had no idea what to do. It brought back memories of my mother and how she handled it when one of us kids were sick.

When I was in third grade, I came home with a slight stomach ache. I went to bed in the same condition; feeling as though I hadn't eaten in days. Mom sat with me for hours, singing to me, or placing a cold cloth on my forehead, her concern and fear unmistakable. When she finally went to bed once she thought I was asleep, I woke up in the middle of the night, the pains worse. Thinking I was hungry, I went downstairs for graham crackers. I remember sitting in what we called the cubbyhole in the upstairs hallway, rocking back and forth in pain while I tried to eat.

The next morning I was no better and stayed home from school. A fever began to soar and Mom researched her medical books, resorting periodically to call a doctor. Unfortunately, Dad was on the night shift and Mom was alone. I remember the tender look on her face as she tried to soothe the pain away. She allowed me to sleep in her bedroom and gave me something to drink. I threw it all up.

Morning came and Dad rushed me to the emergency room. I overheard the doctors telling them that in two more hours I probably would have died. My appendix had burst and infection set in. I was in the hospital for eight days. I wondered if I would be able to handle the emergencies that came my way with this child. Would I be as good a Mother as my own? I hoped so.

When David was born, Dad put a big sign in the yard that said, "IT'S A BOY!" The proud father passed out cigars and gum cigars to anyone who passed by.

George and I agreed that I would stay home after the baby was born. We went to school so we'd be able to open a family day care. I gave my two-week notice on Friday, April 10, 1992, hoping I would have at least two weeks to get ready for this new baby coming. Sarah was born at 9:58 a.m. the next morning.

A Family's Fairytale Turned Upside Down

I spent hours staring at her in awe, pondering how something so perfect came from me. At times, my mind would be spinning, wondering how I could love her so much, because I knew that someday I would lose her.

Having a baby filled so much sadness in my heart. It was one of the happiest days of my life, yet one of the saddest. When George left that night, I looked at my new daughter and let the tears flow. How I wanted my parents to be able to see her, to hold her, to marvel at her. She would never know those special people. It wasn't fair. I raged against God for not allowing them to know one another, to be a part of each other's lives.

As I rocked her, I gazed into her big brown eyes and I didn't know if I could be the Mom she so deserved. How could I be worthy to raise such a beautiful little girl? We took her home and my life changed once again—for the better this time.

Our family day care was coming together. We named it "Big Dreams for Little People," and had all the legal issues worked out, everything was falling into place. I applied for several grants and we were on our way.

Although we had bought a small house next door for the day care it was basically a home business. We had a huge fenced in back yard filled with play equipment. George would open and I would close; a perfect combination for us.

My dreams, however, were shattered in April 1995. That evening we had planned to go grocery shopping when a swat team invaded our street and driveway and entered our home with dogs in tow. I didn't know what was going on, hugging Sarah close to me, terrified. I will admit, at this time, I was smoking marijuana. We never indulged when the kids were in residence, only a joint after work or on the weekends. I didn't know it at the time, but George had a small stalk of marijuana growing in a high, dark cabinet, one I couldn't reach and had no reason to open. Someone apparently let the cat out of the bag and the police swarmed the place, threatening to take Sarah away from me. Terror became my new watchword.

George did spend a thirty days in jail, but I avoided that and the loss of my daughter. However, in June, we had to close the daycare. It wasn't until a few days later that I realized the earth-shattering events in my life all seem to come in June.

Once again, my life was turned upside down. Bitterness of my past and this latest development haunted me.

It was extremely tough letting go of my castle. I worked hard for this dream of owning a small business, but I had to face the facts that I would have to work outside my home to make ends meet. I had once walked away from a horrific car accident and now another fairytale had slipped through my fingers.

I had to control everything around me, not realizing just how little I actually had, but I couldn't let things go. I repeatedly told myself it wasn't as bad as it seemed.

I finally came to the conclusion that if anything were to go right in my life, it would be me taking that control and making it happen. This chapter in my life became my massive pity party and once again, I carried bitterness in my heart.

A Family's Fairytale Turned Upside Down

Losing the daycare tore me apart. Angry, bitter and unforgiving, I chose to hold it all inside me, to hide my pain. My attitude was harsh with a self-righteous attitude.

George had found a job and I had to look for work. The first job I applied for was a receptionist at a local Chiropractic Clinic. I got the job. It started my new career in the office and into the big world of the medical field. Finding a daycare that would fit my specifications for Sarah was an extremely difficult decision to make. My standards were high. I hated that I would miss the milestones in her life and I had to force myself to drop her off and drive away. I finally got a job at the preschool at the church we attended. It was the perfect job, allowing me to care for children and I could take Sarah with me and have the summers off with her.

George and I put the loss and the past behind us. We had good jobs and money was good and we were able to put some aside. Times were getting better, but the neighborhood we lived in was getting worse. We decided to sell our home and the old daycare.

Within three weeks we had sold both homes and moved to a beautiful middle-class neighborhood in Allouez, close to De Pere. The bizarre thing was that it was in the same area I had lived in as a child, when my family was still intact. Was God bringing me closer to home for a reason? I began to wonder what was home—a structure of wood and bricks or a physical and emotional dwelling?

This home was a dream come true. A new beginning. It had a pool, fireplace and a large fenced in back yard. I started to feel my self-worth return for the second time. We were the all American family.

So many wonderful memories are attached to that house. Pool parties, holiday parties, cookouts, we shared it all with our friends. Looking back I wondered why I was falling back into the world—not learning my lesson from losing the daycare.

In 1998, that new beginning was shattered when I received another fateful phone call. Kathy, my beloved older sister, the one I turned to when things got too bad, was sentenced to prison for thirteen years for murder. I wept and mourned for months. In turn I loved her, then hated her in the same breath. I felt she had left me, as well. I'd known her life was spiraling downward. After the courts refused to plea to take the three surviving siblings to live in our own house and raise, the words "unfit," "worthless," "no-good," seemed to imprint themselves in her mind. She'd married, had two children, divorced and spiraled out of control with drugs and alcohol. It didn't appear to matter to the court that her boyfriend had been abusive, that he hurt her more times than I could count. It didn't matter that because she'd been failed by the authorities before, she didn't turn to them in that hour of her need. She did the only thing she knew to do at the moment. And she paid dearly for his death. I came to the conclusion that Kathy had done the crime, so she had to do her time. And I wanted no part of it. She didn't need me anyway—people were there to see that she was taken care of.

In the Fall of 1998, George and I started attending a local Baptist church in Green Bay. We continued going to the weekly Sunday services, but never getting any further involved. Sarah was involved in the AWANA Wednesday night services. I wonder now what kind of message I gave her by sending her to church alone while I stayed home. It had become hard for me to trust anyone in authority and that included the pastor of this church. Getting involved meant commitment and I wasn't ready for that.

Mom and Dad raised us Catholic and I remember Dad taking us to church. We went through all the religious ceremonies and traditions. Unfortunately, I didn't have a clue as to what church was about, or why we did the ceremonies.

The sad part of it all was there was no relationship between the home and the Catholic lifestyle. It was just bold fear of God that we should be good or else. I was told that if I sinned my soul would turn black and that made me feel worse because I had no clue how to make my soul turn bright again.

As I went to confession, I always thought it ridiculous for the person in the other box who would be listening to me and hearing about my sins and all I had to do was recite five Hail Marys and so forth for my sins to be lifted.

We choose to be members of the Baptist church and were baptized on February 28, 1999, We wanted to dedicate our lives to God. Having the opportunity to speak our testimony prior to the actual baptism, I could never get past the point of "I grew up in a very comfortable family atmosphere with two brothers and three sisters. Sad to say at age fourteen, I never had the chance to return home again." I tried to tell myself I had forgiven those who had hurt me so much. I don't think I actually had, but I was good at pretending.

I worked hard at giving Sarah the things I had missed out on after my fourteenth birthday. I'm sure I spoiled her some, but I remembered Dad taking us to Bay Beach in

Green Bay. There you could buy a ride for five cents. On my twelfth birthday, we spent the day at Bay Beach. The best times was when dusk plunged the sky into night and the colored lights of the merry-go-round would come on.

The merry-go-round was my favorite ride. On the ferris wheel an old man took your ticket and made sure you were buckled in properly. As he pulled the lever to make the ferris wheel go around, I noticed his right hand was missing three fingers. I asked him what happened.

"It got caught in the ferris wheel," he said.

Trying to fill my void in Sarah's life, I gave all of myself both physically and emotionally for her. I stretched myself way too thin. I over-extended to make up for her not having grandparents to lavish presents and love upon.

When she turned fourteen, it became impossible for me not to compare our lives. She was so young and innocent. How would she survive if her dad and I were killed? I had to keep reminding myself, I too, was young and innocent and I had survived. Maybe not as well as I would have had things been different, but I was still here and still fighting.

Chapter 12
What Are Memories Really For?

~I will not be defined by the present and future; I needed to hold fast to my memories and pass them along to the next generation~

On June 3, 2001, it was a cold, icy, snowy morning when George left for work. As I was getting myself and Sarah ready for the day, the phone rang. It was St. Vincent's hospital calling to say George was there. He'd been in a car accident.

St. Vincent's Hospital. Twenty-seven years ago, I had entered that same hospital, a scared little girl, not knowing what happened to my family. The thoughts racing through my mind as I rushed down there were of that accident so many years ago. The detail in which I remembered it, floored me. Bloodied glass lying everywhere, on everyone, while David, scared an in pain crawled across my sister's dead body. My emotions were all over the place. Was George okay? I hadn't thought to ask how bad his injuries were, numbed into silence by another tragedy unfolding before me.

Inside, our pastor, Bob, was standing beside George, holding his hand. It gave me some reassurance that George wasn't near death's door or had near-fatal injuries, although he had suffered minor back and neck injuries. He was shaken up, but nothing else seemed to be wrong.

Until he came home. He fell into a deep depression, losing sight of all the goodness in his life. When I would try to hug him, to be close to him, he would mentally pull away and finally I stopped trying.

That old defense mechanism that made me walk to the ambulance that night twenty-seven years ago, raised it's head once again and I realized I could do this by myself, I didn't need anyone—not George, not even God. I was woman—hear me roar.

Once again I was in that valley of death. Church one minute, the liquor store the next. I didn't know what God or anyone else wanted from me and at the moment, I didn't care. This was my life. Either I sucked it up and got on with it, or I wallowed in the self-same dark place George now resided.

I stop seeing my friends. I resented the fact that their lives seemed to always go right, they always had money and I had nothing but a mortgage that needed paying, a nine-year-old daughter, whose demands must be met whether I felt like it or not. And a very depressed husband. The emptiness I had experienced as a child came rushing back.

George's depression didn't improve over the months and I slowly pulled away from him, building a thick wall of self-defense. When anyone asked me how I was, I told them "fine." It was my way of being in control. If no one knew how I felt, then they couldn't feel sorry for me and in feeling sorry for me, they took some of my control away.

I began looking for ways to make extra money. The mortgage still had to be paid, food was essential and the electric bill was non-stop month to month. Something had to be done.

I already worked at the chiropractic office, but I also cleaned houses, worked weekends at a flower shop. I was burning myself out and didn't even know it. I avoided friends, choosing to work instead of party.

A Family's Fairytale Turned Upside Down

George was beyond me it seemed. I pulled further away from him, wanting only to keep food on the table, a roof over our heads and to keep my daughter safe.

A neighbor approached me one day and said I that I was a social butterfly and would make a great bartender. It was another way to help our finances and I found a night job bartending at night.

I was drunk a lot of times at the end of my shift, but that was okay. I was making darn good money and I was having fun. What more could you ask for? I didn't worry about George and Sarah home alone day after day and night after night. In spite of his depression, he was a good Dad and took care of her, taking her to school, picking her up and making sure her needs were met.

My first bartending job, on Mother's Day, of all days, was at Ziggy's supper club. Can anyone say "irony?" I treated my customers well and they returned the favor, filling my tip jar to overflowing. I didn't have a clue how to be a bartender, but I was a quick study and learned by observing fellow bartenders, but I apparently did something right.

One night while tending bar, I heard a woman's voice, crying out, "my ring, my ring." It brought back a vivid memory of my mother. On a Sunday afternoon Mom and Dad had invited the relatives and some friends over for a pool party. The kids were rambunctious and the liner of the pool came loose, collapsing it. Screams filled the air as the huge tidal wave of water exploded from the enclosure, hurtling people everywhere. The impact was so forceful, the water filter was thrown into our neighbor's yard.

I heard Mom crying, "My rug, my rug," as I ran over to her. A large braided rug covered the entire living room and she was worried it would never be the same. After a few minutes, she stopped crying, brushed the tears away and smiled. "You know," said, it's only a rug. Everyone is safe and that's all that matters."

In 2002, we lost another dream home. The bitterness came back. It seemed no matter what I did, nothing ever worked out for me and I was continually losing either those I loved or the things I loved. When did it ever end? Many times as I lay in bed listening to George as he slept, haunting memories would surface. I felt I was being eaten alive from the inside and I had no way of stopping it.

In 2003, I began working at a psychiatric clinic, trying hard to make it work, to be a good employee and to learn the business. I had gotten some of my positive outlook back, but still the doctors saw that I needed help. I began to wonder if there was something seriously wrong with me. In private, I did talk to several of them and I believed every negative thing they had to say.

In the summer of 2003, I began hearing a voice in my head that said, "I love you; it's time." I knew something was about to break and I was afraid it would be me. I knew it was God whispering in my ear, but I didn't know how to let go of all the bitterness, anger and resentment I had built up over the years to let him in. Nor did I trust anything or anyone at this point in my life.

As I struggled with this, I felt an urge to gather information from the courts, the state of Wisconsin and my relatives for answers to the questions I had buried deep inside me. Nobody took the time to share his or her side of the story when asked. I had a lot of uncertainties about my dad's estate, how the material possession had been distributed. Had they sold every single thing my parent's owned? Where were the things that should have rightfully been passed to the surviving children? How had the insurance money been distributed? All these questions raged in my mind and no one would give me honest answers.

Until I walked into my aunt's house and saw possessions that should have been mine or David's or Russell's. They were displayed proudly as though she had a right to them. I confronted them. Got denials and excuses. One thing I wanted more than anything else was my mother's ring. I was denied even that as my aunt said I was not mature enough to take care of it, even though it was plainly stated in my mom's Last Will and Testament. Only George's intervention with threats of lawyers and a court date made them realize they couldn't win on this particular issue. I got the ring, but not much else. They passed away, but yet my parent's possessions that were in their house were not returned to us.

Job: 7---

    I will not be defined only by the present and future; I needed to hold fast to my memories and pass them along to the next generation.

Chapter 13
Delusion of Belonging

~Be careful, do not love anything or anyone above God~

I became disillusioned with bartending. The customers became rude and demanding and while I was there to serve, it wasn't coming from my heart anymore. The same old stories I heard night after night got old very quickly. It became ridiculous career and I started hearing that still, small voice in my ear again saying, "Haven't you had enough? Don't you realize the harm you are causing others?" And I began to think of our car accident and what if that happened again and I had been the one to serve those people? How would that make me feel?

But, on the other hand, I was making enough money to add to the family coffers and if I gave this job up, then we'd be back to nothing. One night I made $52.00 in tips, and the following morning my tire blew and it cost me exactly $52.00 to get another.

It all came to a head one night when a group of people walked in at closing time. It was obvious they were already drunk. An idea popped into my head and I said, "Let me buy you your last drink of the night." They thought that was a great idea. They had apparently been drinking rum and coke so I took out nine glasses, filled them full of ice with straight coke—no rum. Unbelievably, I was told it was the best rum and coke they'd ever had. I began to think of my job as making dirty money and I knew I had to give it up, but the money kept me there in spite of my desire to get away from it.

One Saturday night, a wedding party would be in the bar. The manager gave me instructions on what they wanted to drink and how many there would be. A lump formed in my throat when I realized they would be having Tequila, Rum 151 and Jagermeister. It was the hardest liquor on our shelves and I knew the party would be too drunk to care what happened once they left the bar.

The bride and groom staggered in and she had on one of the most beautiful wedding dresses I'd ever seen. When she turned her back to me, I noticed the dress had a small opening in the back and across her skin was tattooed an upside cross with the devil's face in the middle of the cross. As the night went on, it bothered me more and more. *Hells Bells* was blasting through the speakers and my mind was dizzy with dread.

In the back of the bar, I screwed up the courage and decided this was it. I couldn't stand it any longer. I told the other bartender to keep the tips and I walked out for the last time. As the door closed behind me, a weight lifted off my chest and I could actually breathe again.

Our finances went back to rock-bottom, but even as they asked over and over for me to come back, I refused and I felt good about myself—in control once more. I wasn't sure what I was going to do from here, but anything would be better than the bar.

The idea began formulating in my mind that I wanted to tell my story. I knew other kids had gone through similar circumstances and I felt I should share what had happened to me in order to help others.

A Family's Fairytale Turned Upside Down

In August 2004, I connected with MADD (Mothers Against Drunk Drivers) and got my first speaking engagement. I would be talking to people who had been arrested for the second time for drunk driving. My eighteen-minute story was my way to get out all the hurts, disappointments and anger that I had been harboring for years. The first speaker they had was an offender who had killed two people while driving drunk. He walked up to me after we were finished and knelt before me as he grasped my legs, sobbing intensely and exclaiming how sorry he was for me and that if he could take the pain away, he would. I wasn't sure how to give him any forgiveness. But that night, I did take the first step toward healing. I was a survivor, not a victim and it was a hard lesson for me to learn, but it closed up that hole in my heart just a little more.

A realization so big it staggered me zipped into my head. I had been running in fear from my past and stuffing it down in that small, hidden closet in my mind and refusing to deal with it. After all these years, it was time to let go, and let God. I had finally found the key to unlock all the pain and bitterness and to let it go.

In 2004, I decided to go back to college for an Associates Degree. George had also brought his depression under control and he was in college already. Going to college was a way to go forward, beyond my wildest dreams while healing those numb places in my heart.

One month prior to my graduation, I relieved a letter in the mail from the college. The envelope was fancy and had gold writing on it. I opened it and saw that I had been nominated for Outstanding Student of the Year. I thought it was a joke, but was assured it wasn't and I was requested to be at the recognition dinner.

I was asked to come up with a little speech. I spoke at the dinner and said that "I had never felt like someone—a nobody masquerading as a person." I received a gold-plated solid star that announced I was the outstanding student of the year. What an accomplishment for a nobody like me.

~Psalm 40:2

He lifted me out of the slimy pit, out of the mud and mire; he set; my feet on a rock and gave me a firm place to stand.~NIV

Chapter 14
Victory is Coming

~My childhood marred, I remain steadfast in moving forward step by step and at times I crawl with moments of not moving at all.~

With the door unlocked, I turned my thoughts to Kathy. For eight long years, I let her languish in that prison cell without a word. For some reason, I thought it important that I have my family's blessing to reconnect with her. I called my aunt and she refused to give it. When I told her of decision to return to college for a Bachelor's degree in Psychology, she said I should forget it, that it was way beyond my reach because I wasn't rich enough or smart enough. I didn't bother telling her about the Student of the Year award that I had already received. The words sliced through me like a knife. How dare this woman. After all these years, she still held resentments way beyond my own and I hung up, determined she would no longer have any control over my life.

I wrote a letter to Kathy anyway, pouring out all my frustrations and anger, but also that I loved and missed her and needed her in my life. She still has that letter to this day. And I can thankfully say, our relationship is as strong as it ever was when we were young.

With our relationship tentative at best, I still felt we were getting past the old hurts. It was with great pride that I took a job as a Life Enrichment Specialist for a local assisted living facility. I was finally a part of the community. It was a challenge and I loved it, feeling as though the job fulfilled the healing of my spirit.

So many things had happened to me by this time and I wondered why. What had all the pain, fear, loneliness gotten me? Was I a better person for having experienced it? I don't know and probably never will. I do know it has made me a strong person and that little disappointments in life aren't the major deal they once were. I can let things go, no longer have to have complete control and can turn most every little thing I can't change over to God and let him deal with it. But to what purpose? Another change was about to come my way and I wasn't sure I could handle it, but at the time, I felt I had no choice and it was a way to start all over again, to begin a new chapter in my life. I hoped my future would be better than my past.

George on the other hand, had been talking to his brother in Arkansas who had a remodeling business and needed help. George left for Arkansas in August 2007 and was gone a couple of months. When he came back, he suggested we move to Arkansas. He'd found a place where we could have land and animals, something we'd both wanted for a long time. We discussed it and explained to Sarah about the move. She wasn't very receptive to the change, but we felt we had no choice and decided to move after the first semester of her senior year so she could make friends before the school year started.

We were moving from a town of over 128,000 to one that had less than 400. I felt like a pioneer, but instead of a covered wagon, we'd be moving what few things we kept in a U-Haul with a piercing-eyed Mastodon on the side.

A Family's Fairytale Turned Upside Down

I didn't want to uproot my daughter and leave everything I knew behind, I wanted to sit down and let my emotions take a rest. I had been beaten down, disappointed, afraid and lonely most of my life and now here I was moving halfway across the country where I knew no one.

The morning after we moved into the house we'd rented, we stood on the back deck and looked out over the land. My eyes swept over the beauty Maynard, Arkansas had to offer and I felt I was home.

We found a church in Pocahontas, about 15 miles away and we were welcomed with open arms. The minister, Paster Lynn kindly acknowledged our arrival, stating, "Congregation, please welcome Brother George and his wife and daughter. Let's show them our southern hospitality and help them move into their house after service today."

And they did. Our modern day covered wagon was unloaded in a couple of hours with many helpful hands to get it done. I had never experienced this before. In my past, so many people had said they would help and would either not show up or find excuses not to do anything once they got there. Once they left, it dawned on me. It was Christmas Eve.

We had no stockings hung, no joyous strains of music filling the house, no cookies baking, no decorations. Nothing. I felt empty and sad and my heart went out to Sarah. She didn't deserve this.

I unpacked the nativity display along with a fake Christmas tree with maybe 10 ornaments on it. I was determined to at least acknowledge the day somehow.

That was a life-changing evening as the true meaning of my life finally had purpose. Sarah, when asked if she was happy, replied, "Doesn't matter, we're here, aren't we?" That was the saddest part of the whole move.

I stared at Mary and Joseph, the shepherds on the hill, the three kings standing next to their camels and then, I noticed the manger was empty. I recalled my family's tradition of placing the baby Jesus in the manger on Christmas morning. I glanced at the clock. Midnight.

I realized while sitting there, that Christmas wasn't about present's decorations, partying or friends. It was about love, sharing, helping others and being who I was, who God had made me to be. Was it possible that it was about Jesus' willingness to give his life for us so that we might be saved.

I found baby Jesus in a box, wrapped in gold tissue paper and I unwrapped him and carefully placed him in the manger.

Living in Maynard was certainly an adjustment. The culture of southern living, the slang in the locals voices that I found hard to decipher, sweet tea everywhere you went, and farmlands filled with cows of different varieties. They had a slower pace to life than I was used to. If someone told me they would be out directly, I had no idea if they meant within ten minutes or ten days—or somewhere in between.

Slowly, I learned to shut up and listen while learning—to be still and wait. A Blue Heron helped me learn that lesson as I watched him day after day on one of the ponds on our property. I observed this bird barely moving, waiting patiently for a fish to swim close enough for him to grab. Be still and wait, the reward is coming.

Losing Rufus as I was grieving for my parents and sister was more than I could bear. Up to now, I had shied

A Family's Fairytale Turned Upside Down

away from animals, but here on this farm in Arkansas, I allowed myself to acquire a dog. Four months later, we got a Great Pyrenees puppy I named Rufus in memory of my childhood dog, Rufus.

Life wasn't all fun and games in this new place I now called home. But as I learned the customs and the way of life, I began to see how good it was for me. How it wasn't always a good thing to rush around, to ignore the pain inside. On the back deck, in the early morning hours, I learned a lot about myself. I knew I was still bitter and carried much pride and stubbornness.

I won't say I'm still not a little resentful that God took my family away from me when I was so young, but I know in my heart He had a purpose, a plan. And while I have no idea what that might be, I'm willing to trust Him to see me through.

Chapter 15
Finding Missy's Value

~Jesus paid the price, I'm a princess and heir to the kingdom~

I knew I had a powerful story to tell. And I wanted to share my journey with everyone. I sent out letters to the churches throughout Randolph County, but the only one to respond was Aaron Jarrett, a leader of The Randolph County Celebrate Recovery. This was a program I knew would be good for me and I was ready for a radical change in my life.

When I first started speaking, I still didn't get it. I pointed fingers and I made excuses for my behavior. Finally, a bigger picture started coming through; life and my purpose slowly became less about me and more about God and how He brought me through to the other side.

Weekly, I attended Celebrate Recovery meetings. My purpose for attending these meetings became more than just a healing for me. I could feel my flesh become weakened by the truth of God's love and forgiveness.

As fast as I released my hurts to God, the voids in my heart were immediately filled with truth and life. One of the hardest demons I had to confront and lay down was pride and the feeling that everyone else was messed me, not me. Throughout my years, I had built up a throne for myself and I knew it was crumbling fast. I was able to acknowledge that God's throne was the ultimate power and I was powerless. My broken spirit began to mend only because I began to take my healing seriously. My lowly spirit was elevated and I was able to hold my head up, looking for hopes of restoration. I enjoyed the freedom that came with attending those meetings and I wanted more.

I had cried for years for my fairytale family to return, to be the way it once was. In holding on to that, I missed the good things that were happening right then. I realized that losing over half my family in one split second isn't something anyone could get over quickly.

While my deepest desire was to release the man who caused the accident, I was still angry that he'd only lost his license for a year, that he was instructed not to go to bars and his sentence was only two years for each count of negligent homicide while intoxicated. But, on the other hand, I understood that Jesus died a gruesome death for me had also died for him. I knew that I had to forgive and finally learn to live. By forgiving, I released the torment inside and the hatred began to go away.

I recalled that in our family home there was a large picture of Jesus and I was stared at it for hours. The picture was Jesus standing outside the door waiting for it to open. I realized it was my door, the door to my heart and Jesus waited for me to open it. I had to welcome him into my heart.

For the first time since I was thirteen years old, I felt at peace with myself and I finally forgave the drunk driver who had caused it all. It wasn't easy, but I did it and I felt a peace in my heart I hadn't known for years.

On January 11, 2009, we attended Great Harvest Church in Pocahontas and Keith Carlisle held open the door to the church, smiling with a special kind of love; a soothing look in his eyes that suggested warmth, confidence and love, saying, "Welcome, my friend."

Dottie Cook, a beautiful woman sought me out, intensively looked into my eyes saying welcome, then softly whispered in my ear while hugging me, saying that she loved me. As she walked away, I stood in awe wondering how she can say she loves me, she doesn't even know me. I'm damaged goods and she surely would not love me if she knew my past and my failures. At that moment, I knew she was displaying a unique love known as agape love.

I spent most of my life thinking I wasn't good enough for this or that, that I was not worthy of love, that no matter what I did, nothing would change the fact that I was damaged goods, through no fault of my own, but damaged just the same. When dealing with teenagers, it must be remembered that they take things said literally and if they're told enough times that they don't measure up, soon they'll believe it and it will become a part of them. And they will see no way out, because no one told them they could go to college, could forgive and let it go, could be angry and rail at the world—for awhile—if it helps. But someone must be on hand to tell them they can do anything they want if they want it badly enough. I did. And they can too, but they must have some kind of positive reinforcement for them to believe anything is possible.

I returned to college in spite of my aunt's dire predictions that I wasn't smart enough and enrolled in Williams Baptist College, not far from my new home in Arkansas.

Several courses tore me apart as I began to understand some of my actions and that I had felt the way I should have at various points in my life. Family systems were hard to deal with, and I had to dig deep into the roots of my identity, which was painful and frustrating. One project scared me the most, doing a genogram of my family. I thought of giving up on more than one occasion, but my aunt's voice in my ear and my determination to prove her wrong kept me going. Writing became my passion and in the summer of 2012, I began to write with confidence and clarity. And I realized that some wounds, no matter how hard you try to fix them, simply will not heal. At that point, it's time to cut your losses and get on with your life, leaving those open sores behind.

In May 2012, I graduated with a Bachelors of Science degree in Psychology. It was one of my proudest days and I wanted more than anything to take that diploma to my aunt and wave it in her face and tell her that I *was* smart enough. Maybe not rich enough, but certainly smart enough to follow my dreams and to make something of myself.

Maslow's Hierarchy of needs was evident at this time. My physiological needs, safety, and the true sense of belonging were apparent in my life. My self-esteem started to build up slowly as I was accepted within the community as a person who was able to give back. The education I received was outstanding, thus, giving me the direction to follow my dreams and never give up. My determination to go forward in life became a priority.

Lewis (1960): Unconditional Love/Agape Love

Charity is the love that brings forth caring, regardless of the circumstances. Lewis recognizes this as the greatest of loves, and sees it as a specifically Christian virtue. The chapter on the subject focuses on the need of subordinating the natural loves to the love of God, who is full of charitable love.

Chapter 16
Restored

~I'm not a victim…I'm victorious…~

In February 2012, Kathy suggested it was time to face the mess of our childhood. Her life had spiraled out of control with drugs, abusive boyfriends, and affairs. She spent time in a various institutions and went to prison for murder.

Russell's life hadn't been much better. He had been in a foster home with just a dad, no mother. He'd been going to seminary school before the accident, but afterward, they pulled him out and sent him to public school where he didn't fit in. His legs gave him trouble all his life and still do. He too, had struggled in one way or the other with drugs. He has colon cancer at this writing. All three of us older kids had been alcoholics at some point in our life.

David, we didn't know much about, but I hoped he had been spared that the heartache and pain we had been through. It was time to come together and try to quite the demons that hounded us.

Were all our problems a direct result of losing those so close to us? Or was it a combination of that and the lack of support and the feelings of being unworthy of love that drove us to destructive behavior? I don't know, but I do believe had someone been willing to listen to our needs, our hopes, our sorrow, things could have been different for all three of us.

June 9, 2012. We met at the Allouze Cemetery. We were all apprehensive and nervous. It would be the first time we had all been together, alone, since before the accident.

David spoke first, his voice laced with sorrow. His

gratitude for his journey expressed that no one could change the past, but we could embrace the moments within. That there was a time to let go and move forward.

My turn came and heart beating wildly, I spoke of the pain and bitterness I had carried with me for so many years. And that finally, I had turned it over to God and let it go. My words were simple and humble. But I could not stop smiling as I looked around at my family—finally—standing together.

Russell was next and again, the sorrow and pain came through with his words. He said, "It was nice to get together with the family. Nevertheless, I still feel we were and always will be a broken family. That brokenness lives within me still." He confessed he had wanted to talk to the man who had hit our car that night, but had not done so, afraid of his reaction. The memorial service didn't give Russell the closure I had hoped we would all experience.

Kathy was physically distraught that this was really happening. She expressed the importance of it, to find that closure of unfinished business. She said she had forgiven some people, but mostly, she had forgiven herself. The burden once too heavy to carry had now been lifted.

I found peace that day. It breaks my heart that Russell did not. We poured our hearts out to each other and the service was not in vain. On that day, Kathy, Russell, David and I had a chance to say goodbye and finally to release the past and let it go. I pray that one day Russell will find that same peace.

The fairytale I once had ended in a shattering of glass and shriek of metal on metal. Today, I carry no more shame, guilt or dishonor. I was meant to survive when others in my family did not. I don't know why, but the why doesn't matter. We'll never know the answers to those kinds of questions here on Earth. I am confident, happy and living with a man I found true love with and it is good.

Through the years, God came and went in my life. Sometimes I was angry at him for taking everything I cared about away from me. Sometimes I leaned on Him when I didn't even realize I was doing it. And sometimes, I actively sought His love and protection. No matter where I was in life, I did believe in God and though it took many years and many heartaches—He brought me through and I know He was with me on the entire journey. I am blessed.

One of the biggest journeys in my life has ended, but another have come on January 24, 2012. George Alberts, my helpmate, spouse and friend has Alzheimer's.

Do not allow the devil to steal good memories from you; keep them alive in your heart forever.

The promise of Heaven is not a fairytale. The only true happy ending is eternity with Jesus Christ.

Maslow's Hierarchy of needs is once again complete as it was in my childhood. I have a wonderful home where I feel safe, freedom from fear of the world around me. The belonging and love I feel is beyond anything I have felt before. My self-esteem remains high due to my simple achievements. I have gained the respect of others and I feel the same respect in return. Having written this book and given the ability to offer hope to others has given me self-actualization beyond my wildest dreams.

In anyone's lifetime, the Maslow's Hierarchy of needs will change due to unexpected circumstances. Loss of anything such as a job, house, pet or loved one will affect the family system and throw it out of balance. From my experiences, change and transition is a process and not always easy. Once the balance returns, the Hierarchy of needs will adjust as well.

Care: Generativity vs. Stagnation (Middle adulthood, 25-64, or 40-64 years)

- **Existential Question: Can I Make My Life Count?**

<u>Generativity</u> is the concern of guiding the next generation. Socially-valued work and disciplines are expressions of generativity. Simply having or wanting children does not in and of itself achieve generativity.

During middle age the primary developmental task is one of contributing to society and helping to guide future generations. In contrast, a person who is self-centered and unable or unwilling to help society move forward develops a feeling of stagnation- a dissatisfaction with the relative lack of productivity.

My Christ did not hide his scars on his hand, the scars were very visible as a sign of victory. Just like your hurts and your scars either physical or emotional, are your victories through Jesus Christ. Every scar that I bear is my personal testimony. Everyone carries scars; do not waste what lessons you have learned.

~Romans 5: 3, 4

Not only so, but we also rejoice in our sufferings, because we know that suffering produces perseverance; perseverance, character; and character, hope.~

Please visit my website at www.FamilyFairytale.org

I am available for speaking engagements that can assist with various in-service, events, conferences and conventions. Bookings may be booked one year in advance. Please contact me at Familyfairytale060974@yahoo.com or 920-562-0365. Text is acceptable.

- Mental health and Medical services
- Teen services
- School functions and assemblies
- Colleges
- Retreat Centers
- Loss and Grief Support Groups
- Women and Youth church groups
- Recovery Groups
- Rehab Centers
- Prisons
- Juvenile Court/delinquency

Book trailer on YouTube/www.FamilyFairytale.org or www.youtube.com/user/MockingBirdlanePress

References

Baird, Abigail A. (2011). *Think Psychology*. New Jersey: Person Education, Inc.

Cline, F., Fay J. (2006). *Parenting with Love & Logic*. Colorado Springs: NavPress.

Maslow, A. (1987). *Motivation and Personality*. New York: Harper Press.

McMahan, I. (2009). *Adolescence*. New Jersey: Pearson Education, Inc.

Richardson, R. (1995). *Family Ties That Bind* Canada: International Self-Counsel Press Ltd.

CPSIA information can be obtained at www.ICGtesting.com
Printed in the USA
LVOW130816190613

339250LV00003B/9/P